Autumn Gatherings

Autumn Gatherings

Casual Food to Enjoy with Family and Friends

Rick Rodgers

Photographs by Ben Fink

WILLIAM MORROW

An Imprint of HarperCollins Publishers

HarperCollins books may be purchased for educational, business, or sales promotional use. For information please write: Special Markets Department, HarperCollins Publishers, 10 East 53rd Street, New York, NY 10022.

FIRST EDITION

Designed by Lorie Pagnozzi

Library of Congress Cataloging-in-Publication Data has been applied for.

ISBN 978-0-06-143884-4

08 09 10 11 12   OV/RRD   10 9 8 7 6 5 4 3 2 1

 # Acknowledgments

Whether you are building a house or writing books, some projects just go more smoothly than others. In the case of this book, and its companions, I was surrounded by people whose company I truly enjoy. From brainstorming the various recipe ideas and photographing them to developing the book's look, we had as much fun as hard work.

First and foremost, I am grateful to David Sweeney at HarperCollins for his invitation to create the Seasonal Gatherings series. Gail Winston edited the book with a sure, but sensitive, hand. Sarah Whitman-Salkin was a magnificent ringmaster, keeping communications between David, Gail, myself, and many other players under control. Thanks again to Sonia Greenbaum for copyediting another one of my books. I am especially thankful for the beautiful work of Lorie Pagnozzi, the series' designer. Susan Ginsburg and I have been close friends for more than twenty-five years. When we first met, neither of us could have foreseen that one day we would be agent and client. We have spent many autumns together, and I hope that there are many more ahead. And Bethany Stout, Susan's lovely assistant, is simply indispensable.

Photographer Ben Fink and I started out as colleagues and now we're friends. I hope he enjoyed the time we spent photographing the food. Jamie Kimm and Roy Finamore lent their excellent styling skills (food and props, respectively) to the jacket photograph. And a special thanks to Joe Tully, who generously turned over the gorgeous home he shares with Ben for our photo sessions. Arlene Ward and Josine Spina of Adventures in Cooking in Wayne, New Jersey, and the staff of Sur La Table in Livingston, New Jersey, generously loaned their tableware.

In my own home, my longtime assistant and friend, Diane Kniss, got me through another book with her laughter and efficiency. Michelle Grevesen jumped in to help out and did a great job. Many friends contributed recipes and ideas: Barbara Caccavella, Skip Dye, Linda West Eckhardt, Priscila Satakoff, and Marguerite Scandiffio. As usual, Patrick Fisher lent his finely tuned palate to taste-testing, and didn't gain an ounce.

Contents

Introduction

We all have friends who start announcing the shortening of daylight as soon as they come back from summer vacation. "Look how soon it's getting dark!" As soon as the temperature drops a degree, they remark, "Oh, it's going to be an early winter!" When tomatoes and basil dwindle at the farmers' market, they lament. They act as if summer is the only season that is worthwhile. Not so . . .

When I notice a nip in the air, I don't complain. I welcome the change in the temperature and humidity, the coloring of the leaves, the mums in the garden. But most of all, I rejoice in cooking with the season's produce.

This is the season of some of my favorite fruits and vegetables. When I was growing up in California, my suburban hometown still showed its agrarian roots with farm stands along the roads and with old fruit trees growing in backyards. Autumn meant a variety of fruits and vegetables that were entirely different from the summer bounty but no less delicious: puckery pomegranates (to eat one, Mom made me wear an old shirt that could take the staining juice); honeyed persimmons that Grandma Rodgers would transform into cookies; sticky-sweet figs that would ripen on the tree and drop to the ground so we never had to pick them; tart, thick-skinned lemons for the best lemon desserts you ever had.

I had never bought persimmons, figs, or lemons until I left California and moved to New York City. I was shocked at the price I had to pay for that first lemon. To this day, transplanted Californians are never happier than when we get a box of lemons (preferably Meyer) mailed from home. (Well, unless you send us a box of See's candies, but I digress.) And when I moved east, I discovered a whole new world of fall favorites particular to the region, including earthy parsnips, juicy apples, and foxy Concord grapes.

As the weather turns cooler, we cook differently, too. Instead of grilling outdoors to keep the kitchen cool, I look for recipes for roasting, baking, and braising. These warm the kitchen with heat from the stove and fill the house with rich aromas as well. After a summer with a parade of vegetable-based salads, I really look forward to that first bowl of rib-sticking chili or an Oktoberfest dinner of sausages simmered in red cabbage. These slow-cooked dishes are perfect for weekend entertaining, and many of them are even better when made a day or two ahead and reheated.

Although my close circle of friends includes many incredible cooks, both professional and untrained, when we get together, you might be surprised at the food we serve. Invariably, the dishes are delicious but simply prepared. The main course might be an artful, long-braised stew or a no-fuss roast surrounded by vegetables that pick up the meat's flavor. Our shared time is about being together, not about how many pots and pans are dirtied. We have learned how to make food that is packed with flavor but doesn't always call for lots of work in the kitchen. And cooking with produce at the peak of its flavor is one surefire way to make your meals as tasty as possible.

While *Autumn Gatherings* is about casual meals to share with your friends—and about encouraging your friends and family to use the best seasonal produce—let's not forget two important autumn holidays at which food plays a big role: Halloween and Thanksgiving. There's obviously more to Halloween food than trick-or-treat candy, as recent statistics show that it is the number one holiday for party-giving. You'll find some ideas here for your party's menu (although I will tell you up front that I personally don't go for grotesque decorations and prefer just to serve lots of good food without silly garnishes). And, of course, Thanksgiving is about traditions, but I'm offering some dishes that are brightened with contemporary flavors, along with a wonderful roast turkey. And don't ignore the other events that make the season unique. You'll find recipes for a tailgate cookout, and even an Oktoberfest supper. (I may put a little more emphasis on the latter because my great-uncle Bill was the leader of an oompah band and produced our local Oktoberfest, where I worked selling sausages with my cousins.)

In the food-writing business, in order to satisfy deadlines months before publication, I sometimes have to cook with out-of-season ingredients. Now, you can get just about anything you can imagine every day of the year at my local supermarkets—but that doesn't mean that it will have any flavor. Being forced to create a summer recipe with peaches in November made me realize how I longed to return to the parsnips, cranberries, and potatoes I had just bought at the farm stand. In this book, I use produce in the traditional harvest cycles, not in the modern "it's always summer somewhere" mentality. Even if you add variety to your meals with Holland red peppers in November, I encourage you to cook with sustainable, local foods as much as you can. Your food will be so much better for it.

APPETIZERS AND BEVERAGES

Buttermilk Focaccia with Gorgonzola and Grapes

French Onion Galette

Autumn Fruits with Prosciutto and Aged Balsamico

Warm Roasted Butternut Squash Salsa with Tortilla Chips

White Bean Dip with Roasted Garlic

Smoked Salmon Salad on Belgian Endive

Hot Buttered Apple Cider

Buttermilk Focaccia with Gorgonzola and Grapes

My friend Joel Roark is a great baker. At a dinner at his house recently, he served the lightest, fluffiest focaccia I've ever had. I snagged the recipe, which was originally his late mother's. Buttermilk may not be the most authentic Italian ingredient (I suspect that Mrs. Roark reworked a dinner roll recipe for her flatbread), but it makes wonderful focaccia, especially for this sweet and savory rendition.

FOCACCIA DOUGH

¾ cup buttermilk

3 tablespoons extra-virgin olive oil, plus more for the bowl, pan, and topping

1 teaspoon sugar

1 teaspoon salt

¼ teaspoon baking soda

One ¼-ounce package active dry yeast

1 tablespoon warm (105° to 115°F) water

2½ cups unbleached flour, as needed

2 cups seedless red grapes, vertically cut in halves

1 cup (4 ounces) crumbled Gorgonzola (see Note)

Freshly ground black pepper

1. To make the focaccia dough, warm the buttermilk in a small saucepan over low heat or in a microwave oven just until it loses its chill. Transfer to the bowl of a heavy-duty electric mixer. Add the oil, sugar, salt, and baking soda and stir.

2. Sprinkle the yeast over the warm water in a very small bowl and let stand until the yeast softens, about 5 minutes. Stir well to dissolve the yeast and pour into the mixer bowl.

3. Affix the paddle attachment to the mixer and turn the mixer on low speed. Gradually add enough of the flour to make a slightly sticky dough that pulls away from the side of the bowl. Switch the paddle attachment to the dough hook. Mix on medium-low speed to knead the dough until it is soft and supple, about 7 minutes.

4. Transfer the dough to an oiled medium bowl and turn to coat the dough with oil. Cover the bowl tightly with plastic wrap. Let stand in a warm, draft-free place until the dough is doubled in volume, about 1 $\frac{1}{2}$ hours.

5. Position a rack in the center of the oven and preheat the oven to 375°F. Lightly oil a 15 x 10 x 1-inch jelly roll pan.

6. Meanwhile, punch down the dough and transfer it to the oiled pan. Stretch and pat out the dough to fit the pan. (If the dough retracts, cover it with plastic wrap, let it relax for about 5 minutes, and try again.) Cover the dough with plastic wrap and let stand until puffed, about 30 minutes.

7. Scatter the grapes over the the top of the focaccia, leaving a 1-inch-wide border on all four sides. Sprinkle the Gorgonzola over the grapes. Brush the border with olive oil.

8. Bake until the focaccia is golden brown, about 20 minutes. Transfer the pan to a wire cake rack and let cool until warm, about 10 minutes. Grind a generous amount of black pepper over the focaccia. Cut into thirds lengthwise, then crosswise into eighths to make 24 pieces. Serve warm or cooled to room temperature.

Note

Domestic Gorgonzola, which has a firmer texture and crumbles more readily than the Italian varieties, works best for this recipe. Any firm blue cheese can be substituted.

This recipe is also great with Concord grapes, but the seeds must be removed after the grapes are cut in half.

French Onion Galette

A galette is a savory free-form tart, and it is one of the most versatile of all appetizers, as it can be served with drinks before dinner or with salad as a first course. This version, with lots of caramelized onions and nutty Gruyère, is reminiscent of French onion soup. Try it with a glass of Beaujolais nouveau.

2 tablespoons unsalted butter

2 large onions, cut into thin half-moons

Salt and freshly ground black pepper

Perfect Butter Pastry Dough (page 140)

1½ cups (6 ounces) shredded Gruyère cheese

1 teaspoon chopped fresh thyme

1. Position a rack in the bottom third of the oven and preheat the oven to 400°F.

2. Melt the butter in a large skillet over medium heat. Add the onions, stir well, and cover. Cook, stirring occasionally, until the onions soften, about 6 minutes. Uncover and reduce the heat to medium-low. Cook, stirring often, until the onions are very tender and golden, about 25 minutes. Season with salt and pepper to taste. Cool completely.

3. On a lightly floured work surface, roll out the dough into a 12- to 13-inch-diameter round about ⅛ inch thick. Slide onto a large rimless baking sheet (or the bottom of an inverted rimmed baking sheet). Sprinkle half of the Gruyère over the dough,

6   AUTUMN GATHERINGS

leaving a 1½-inch-wide border. Spread the onions over the cheese, then sprinkle with the remaining cheese. Working around the perimeter of the galette, fold the border of exposed dough up and over, pleating it as you go, leaving the onions exposed.

4. Bake until the dough is golden brown on the bottom (lift up an edge to check), 25 to 30 minutes. Cool slightly, then cut into wedges. Sprinkle the tart with the thyme. Serve warm or cooled to room temperature on cocktail plates with forks.

A Halloween Party

Persimmons

You will find two kinds of these bright orange fruits at your market, and be forewarned that they are not the same.

Hachiya persimmons are the larger of the two, with a smooth, bulbous shape. Ripening at room temperature is a very important step with Hachiya persimmons, as a fruit eaten before its time will be very unpleasantly tannic. A ripe fruit is actually squishy, and it will take on a translucent look. Do not be afraid to let it ripen this far! Hachiya is the variety to use for making cookies, cakes, and the like. Cut off the green calyx at the top of the very ripe persimmon, cut the flesh into chunks (discarding any seeds that you might come across), and puree in a food processor or blender. The puree freezes well for a few months, so it may be more convenient to ripen, puree, and freeze a quantity of persimmons and then thaw a small amount of puree as needed.

Fuyu persimmons are squat, with a few indentations in their curves. These do not need long ripening and should be eaten when firm, or firm-ripe. They will never ripen until they are squishy, and they don't make good puree for baking. Just cut off the calyx, cut the fruit into thin slices, and enjoy raw as a snack or in salads.

Autumn Fruits
with Prosciutto and
Aged Balsamico

Makes 6 servings

This requires no actual recipe, but it is worth outlining for those cooks who may not be familiar with some of the components. And it is one of my favorite first courses, showing that autumn's fruits can be every bit as delicious as anything that summer has to offer. If you are not serving this to close friends, leave off the Concord grapes, or use the more boring but etiquette-approved seedless ones. For sensational results, use the best imported prosciutto di Parma (which is more delicate than most domestic versions) and top-notch balsamico.

1 Asian pear, cored and cut into 12 wedges

2 large figs, each cut into 6 wedges

2 Fuyu persimmons, calyx removed, each cut into 6 wedges

6 ounces Concord grapes, separated into 6 small bunches

6 ounces thinly sliced prosciutto, preferably prosciutto di Parma

Balsamic vinegar, preferably an aged artisan balsamico,
    for drizzling (see Note)

1. For each serving arrange 2 slices each of the Asian pear, figs, and persimmons, and 1 bunch of grapes, around the perimeter of each of 6 dinner plates. Drape equal amounts of the prosciutto in the center of each plate, letting the slices fall to create a mound.

2. Drizzle the vinegar around the fruit and prosciutto and serve immediately.

Note

Aged balsamic vinegar, which is made in small batches by dedicated Italian artisans, has a much more complex flavor and thicker consistency than supermarket balsamic. You'll find it at specialty food stores and online. In a pinch, you can make a balsamic glaze from inexpensive vinegar, which is one-dimensional but acceptable. Boil 1/2 cup balsamic vinegar in a small saucepan until it is thick, syrupy, and reduced to about 3 tablespoons. Cool completely.

Warm Roasted Butternut Squash Salsa with Tortilla Chips

Makes about 4 cups

One autumn night, I made a vegetarian chili with a fall favorite, roasted butternut squash. When I served it with tortilla chips, I realized that with a few adjustments, it would make a great dip for a Halloween party. Keep it warm in a mini–slow cooker, or try it cooled to room temperature, served in a hollowed pumpkin.

1½ pounds butternut squash, peeled, seeded, and cut into ½-inch chunks

3 tablespoons extra-virgin olive oil, divided

1 onion, diced

1 red bell pepper, seeded and cored, cut into ¼-inch dice

2 garlic cloves, minced

1 jalapeño pepper, seeded and minced

One 14½-ounce can diced tomatoes, drained

One 15- to 19-ounce can pinto beans, drained and rinsed

1 zucchini, cut into ½-inch dice

2 tablespoons chopped fresh cilantro

¼ cup coarsely chopped shelled and toasted pumpkin seeds (pepitas)

Salt and pepper

Tortilla chips, for serving

1. Position a rack in the center of the oven and preheat the oven to 400°F. Lightly oil a baking sheet.

2. Toss the squash with 1 tablespoon of the oil and spread on a rimmed baking sheet. Roast, stirring occasionally, until the squash is lightly browned and tender, about 25 minutes.

3. Meanwhile, heat the remaining 2 tablespoons of oil in a large skillet or saucepan over medium-high heat. Add the onion, bell pepper, garlic, and jalapeño and cook, stirring occasionally, until the onion is golden, about 8 minutes. Add the tomatoes, beans, zucchini, and cilantro and cook, stirring occasionally, until the zucchini is crisp-tender, about 5 minutes. Stir in the roasted squash and cook for 5 minutes more. (The salsa can be roasted, cooled, covered, and refrigerated up to 3 days ahead. Reheat over medium heat, stirring occasionally.) Stir in the pumpkin seeds. Season with salt and pepper.

4. Transfer to a mini—slow cooker and serve warm with the tortilla chips.

White Bean Dip with Roasted Garlic

Makes about 3 cups

Roasted garlic is a great way to add flavor to dips, soups, and other dishes; about the only thing I haven't tried it on is chocolate cake. This dip will make your Halloween party rock.

1 large head garlic

½ cup extra-virgin olive oil, plus more for drizzling

Salt and freshly ground black pepper

Two 15- to 19-ounce cans white beans (cannellini), drained and rinsed

2 tablespoons fresh lemon juice

1 tablespoon chopped fresh rosemary (optional)

Crackers or pita crisps, for serving

1. Preheat the oven to 400°F. Cut the top from the garlic head to make a lid. Drizzle a little oil over the bottom half, season with a pinch of salt and pepper, then replace the lid to return the garlic to its former shape. Wrap the head in foil. Place the garlic on a baking sheet and bake until it is tender and golden, about 40 minutes. Let cool. Squeeze the garlic flesh out of the hulls.

2. Place the roasted garlic, beans, and lemon juice in a food processor fitted with the metal blade. With the machine running, slowly add the ½ cup oil and process until smooth. Add the rosemary, if using. Season to taste with salt and pepper, and pulse to combine. (The dip can be made up to 3 days ahead, covered, and refrigerated.) Transfer to a serving bowl and serve at room temperature with the crackers.

Smoked Salmon Salad on Belgian Endive

Mildly bitter Belgian endive is often called on to act as a cup to hold savory ingredients for an appetizer. This is a great snack to serve before a heavy meal because it is light but flavorful. If you find red Belgian endive, use it in combination with the familiar ivory-colored leaves.

SMOKED SALMON SALAD

2 teaspoons fresh lemon juice

2 tablespoons extra-virgin olive oil

4 ounces sliced smoked salmon, cut across the grain into ¼-inch-wide strips

¼ cup peeled, seeded, and minced cucumber

1 small scallion, white and green parts, minced

Salt and freshly ground black pepper

2 Belgian endive, separated into 24 leaves

Finely chopped chives, for garnish

1. To make the salad, whisk together the lemon juice and oil in a medium bowl. Add the smoked salmon, cucumber, and scallion and mix gently. Season lightly with salt and pepper to taste. (The salad can be prepared up to 1 hour ahead, covered, and refrigerated.)

2. Spoon equal amounts of the salad into the wide ends of the endive leaves. Garnish with the chives. Serve chilled.

Hot Buttered Apple Cider

Makes 8 servings

Curling up with a good book and a cup of hot cider on a chilly afternoon is the kind of activity that makes cold weather (almost) welcome. This version is spicier than most and will really warm you to the bone.

6 quarter-sized slices peeled fresh ginger

6 star anise

Four 3-inch-long cinnamon sticks, plus more for garnish

1 teaspoon whole cloves

1 teaspoon fennel seed

1 teaspoon Sichuan peppercorns

1 quart fresh apple cider

Calvados or applejack, for serving (optional)

8 tablespoons (1 stick) unsalted butter, cut into tablespoons

1. Rinse and squeeze out a 12-inch square of cheesecloth. Wrap the ginger, star anise, cinnamon, cloves, fennel seed, and Sichuan peppercorns in the cheesecloth. Using a piece of kitchen twine, tie it into a packet.

2. Pour the cider in a large nonreactive saucepan and add the spice bundle. Bring to a simmer over medium-low heat, stirring occasionally.

3. Ladle the cider into warmed mugs. Add a dry cinnamon stick to each mug, and spike with Calvados. Top each with a pat of butter. Serve hot.

SOUPS AND SALADS

Butternut Squash Bisque with Chipotle–Red Pepper Swirl

Broccoli and Roasted Garlic Soup

Ham, Yam, and Kale Soup

Golden Cauliflower and Cheddar Soup

Turkey Chowder with Wild Rice, Cremini, and Pancetta

Celery Root and Red Pepper Slaw

Pear, Pomegranate, and Greens Salad

Carrot, Cranberry, and Walnut Salad

Cauliflower Salad with Parsley-Caper Vinaigrette

Butternut Squash Bisque with Chipotle–Red Pepper Swirl

Makes 6 to 8 servings

The Day-Glo golden color of this butternut squash bisque is sure to make your mouth water with anticipation. This soup gets its luscious texture not from cream but from the rice simmered with the vegetables. To set the bisque off even more, add a splash of chipotle-spiced pureed red pepper, adjusting the amount of chile to match your guests' heat tolerance.

CHIPOTLE–RED PEPPER PUREE

1 large red bell pepper

1 teaspoon adobo sauce from canned chipotle chiles, or more to taste (see Note)

BISQUE

2 tablespoons unsalted butter

1 medium onion, chopped

1 medium carrot, chopped

1 medium celery rib, chopped

2 garlic cloves, finely chopped

2¼ pounds butternut squash, peeled, seeded, and cut into 1-inch cubes

4 cups canned low-sodium chicken broth

⅓ cup long-grain rice

Salt and freshly ground black pepper

1. To make the puree, position the broiler rack 6 inches from the source of heat and preheat the broiler. Cut the top and bottom from the bell pepper to make "lids." Slice

the pepper lengthwise and open it up. Cut out and discard the ribs and seeds. Place the opened pepper with its top and bottom, skin side up, on the rack. Broil until the skin is blackened, about 8 minutes. Transfer to a bowl and cover. Let stand for 10 minutes. Remove and discard the blackened peel. Puree the red pepper and adobo sauce in a blender, adding more adobo to taste. Transfer to a small bowl, cover, and refrigerate until ready to use. (The puree can be made up to 5 days ahead.)

2. To make the bisque, heat the butter in a soup pot over medium heat. Add the onion, carrot, and celery and cover. Cook the vegetables, stirring occasionally, until they are softened, about 5 minutes. Stir in the garlic and cook uncovered until it gives off its aroma, about 1 minute. Add the squash and stir well. Add the broth and rice and bring to a boil over high heat. Reduce the heat to medium-low. Cover and simmer until the squash is very tender, about 25 minutes. Season with salt and pepper to taste.

3. In batches, in a blender with the lid ajar, puree the vegetables and broth and transfer to a warmed soup tureen. (Or use a handheld immersion blender to puree in the pot.) Serve in individual bowls, drizzling the red pepper puree over each serving.

Note

I used to have to go to a Latino grocer to get canned chipotle chiles. Now they are sold at my local supermarket. Smoked jalapeño chiles packed in a spicy chile puree called adobo, they add a jolt of smoky hot flavor to food. After opening, transfer the leftover chiles to a small airtight container and store in the refrigerator, where they will keep for a month or so. Or, place the individual chiles with their clinging sauce on a waxed paper–lined baking sheet, and freeze the chiles until they are solid. Put the frozen chiles in a zippered plastic bag and freeze for up to 3 months.

Broccoli and Roasted Garlic Soup

Makes 6 to 8 servings

Roasted garlic is a great thing to have in the refrigerator, ready to perk up your everyday cooking. I often take a few seconds to prepare a couple of heads and toss them in the oven when I am roasting something else. One autumn Saturday afternoon, when I wanted a warming soup after gardening, I made this soup from what was at hand, and now it's a staple.

ROASTED GARLIC

1 large, plump head garlic

Olive oil, for drizzling

Salt and freshly ground black pepper

1 large bunch broccoli, about 1¾ pounds

2 tablespoons unsalted butter

1 medium onion, chopped

1 large baking potato, such as russet or Burbank, peeled and cut into 1-inch chunks

6 cups canned low-sodium chicken broth

1. Position a rack in the center of the oven and preheat to 400°F.

2. To roast the garlic, cut off the top ½ inch of the garlic head to make a "lid." Drizzle the cut surfaces with a little olive oil and season with a pinch each of salt and pepper. Replace the lid to return the garlic to its original shape. Wrap the garlic in aluminum foil and place on a baking sheet. Bake until the garlic is deep beige and tender, about 45 minutes. Unwrap and cool.

3. Cut the florets from the broccoli stalks and coarsely chop the florets. Pare and coarsely chop the stalks.

4. Melt the butter in a large saucepan over medium heat. Add the onion and cover. Cook, stirring often, until the onion is tender, about 5 minutes. Stir in the chopped broccoli florets and stalks and the potato. Add the broth and bring to a boil over high heat. Reduce the heat to low and partially cover the pot. Simmer until the potato is very tender, about 30 minutes. During the last 5 minutes, squeeze the roasted garlic from the hulls into the pot, discarding the hulls. Season with salt and pepper to taste.

5. In batches, puree the soup in a blender with the lid ajar. (Or use a handheld immersion blender to puree in the pot.) Serve hot.

Ham, Yam, and Kale Soup

Makes 8 servings

Whenever I am in the south, I head to one of the local cafeterias for a dinner of ham, yams, and smothered greens. Back home, I turn the tasty trio into a rib-sticking soup. The ham and vegetables will lend plenty of flavor to the cooking liquid, so don't bother to use more than a couple of cups of chicken broth. Cranberry and Sage Cornbread (page 115) would be great with this.

One 1¼-pound ham steak

2 tablespoons vegetable oil

1 medium onion, chopped into ½-inch dice

1 medium carrot, chopped into ½-inch dice

1 medium celery rib, chopped into ½-inch dice

2 garlic cloves, finely chopped

2 orange-fleshed yams, such as Louisiana, garnet, or jewel, peeled and
   cut into 1-inch pieces

4 cups packed shredded curly kale

2 cups canned low-sodium chicken broth

¼ teaspoon crushed hot red pepper

Salt and freshly ground black pepper

1. Trim the outer layer of fat from the perimeter of the ham steak, and chop the fat. Cut the ham into bite-size pieces and reserve the ham bone.

2. Heat the fat and oil together in a soup pot over medium-low heat until the ham fat begins to melt, about 5 minutes. Add the onion, carrot, celery, and garlic and stir well. Cover and cook until the vegetables soften, about 10 minutes.

3. Stir in the ham and ham bone, then the yams and kale. Add 6 cups water, the broth, and the hot red pepper and bring to a boil over high heat. Return the heat to medium-low and partially cover the pot. Simmer until the yams are tender but not falling apart, about 40 minutes. Season with salt and pepper to taste.

4. Ladle into bowls and serve hot.

Golden Cauliflower and Cheddar Soup

Golden cauliflower has the warm shade of a harvest-time sunset. Unlike some other unusually colored vegetables, this one doesn't turn pale after cooking. Cheddar cheese adds its sharp flavor to the soup and matches the soup's color, too.

2 tablespoons unsalted butter

1 medium onion, chopped

1 medium carrot, chopped

1 medium celery rib, chopped

2 pounds golden cauliflower, coarsely chopped

5 cups canned low-sodium chicken broth

1 cup (4 ounces) shredded sharp Cheddar cheese

2 teaspoons cornstarch

Salt and freshly ground black pepper

1. Melt the butter in a soup pot over medium heat. Add the onion, carrot, and celery and cover. Cook, stirring occasionally, until the vegetables soften, about 5 minutes.

2. Stir in the cauliflower and the broth. Cover and bring to a boil over high heat. Reduce the heat to medium-low and simmer until the cauliflower is very tender, about 30 minutes.

3. Toss together the Cheddar and cornstarch in a bowl to coat the cheese. A handful at a time, stir into the simmering soup, and cook until the cheese is melted and the soup is lightly thickened. Do not boil. Season with salt and pepper to taste. Serve hot.

Turkey Chowder with Wild Rice, Cremini, and Pancetta

Makes 12 servings

The time-honored post-Thanksgiving tradition of Friday turkey soup is almost as entrenched as the roasted turkey itself. Great turkey soup is a two-step process. First make a hearty broth with just the turkey carcass. From there, create a hearty chowder that will stand as a meal on its own.

ROASTED TURKEY BROTH

1 turkey carcass, from a 12- to 15-pound roasted turkey, including skin

2 tablespoons vegetable oil

1 medium onion, chopped

1 medium carrot, chopped

1 medium celery rib with leaves, chopped

4 parsley sprigs

½ teaspoon dried thyme

¼ teaspoon black peppercorns

1 bay leaf

Salt and freshly ground black pepper

CHOWDER

¾ cup wild rice, rinsed and drained

1 tablespoon vegetable oil

6 ounces thick-sliced pancetta or bacon, diced

12 ounces cremini (baby bella) mushrooms, sliced

4 tablespoons (½ stick) unsalted butter

2 medium carrots, diced

2 medium celery ribs, diced

½ cup chopped shallots

⅓ cup all-purpose flour

2½ quarts Roasted Turkey Broth

1 teaspoon dried rosemary

4 cups (about 1 pound) bite-size diced turkey, cooked

1½ cups thawed frozen corn kernels

1 cup heavy cream

Salt and freshly ground black pepper

Chopped fresh parsley, for garnish

1. To make the broth, cut off the edible turkey meat from the carcass and cut it into bite-size pieces. Cover and refrigerate while making the soup. Rinse the carcass under cold running water to remove clinging stuffing and glaze, if needed. Break, tear, and chop the carcass into large pieces.

2. Heat the oil in large stockpot over medium heat. Add the onion, carrot, and celery and cover. Cook until softened, about 5 minutes. Add the carcass pieces and add enough cold water to barely cover (about 3½ quarts). Bring to a boil over high heat, skimming off any foam that rises to the surface. Add the parsley, thyme, peppercorns, and bay leaf. Reduce the heat to low and simmer, partially covered, adding hot water as needed to keep the bones submerged, for 3 hours.

3. Strain the broth into a large bowl, pressing hard on the solids. Let stand for 5 minutes, then skim off the fat from the surface. Season with salt and pepper to taste. Makes about 2½ quarts broth.

4. To make the chowder, bring 2½ cups water, ¼ teaspoon salt, and the wild rice to a boil in a medium saucepan. Cover and reduce heat to low. Simmer until the wild rice is tender, 45 to 60 minutes, depending on the variety of wild rice. (Hand-harvested wild rice from the Great Lakes usually takes longer than the machine-harvested California variety.) Drain in a wire sieve, if necessary. Set aside.

5. Meanwhile, heat the oil in a soup pot over medium heat. Add the pancetta and cook, stirring occasionally, until browned, about 8 minutes. Using a slotted spoon, transfer the pancetta to paper towels to drain. Add the cremini to the pot and cook, stirring often, until beginning to brown, about 8 minutes. Transfer to a bowl.

6. Add the butter to the pot and melt. Add the carrots and celery and cover. Cook, stirring often, until softened, about 5 minutes. Stir in the shallots and cook until softened, about 2 minutes. Sprinkle in the flour and stir well. Return the cremini to the pot. Stir in the broth and rosemary. Bring to a boil, stirring often, over high heat. Reduce the heat to medium-low. Simmer, partially covered, for 15 minutes. Add the wild rice, turkey, corn, and pancetta. Cook until the turkey is heated through, about 10 minutes. Stir in the cream and heat without boiling. Season with salt and pepper to taste. (The soup can be cooled, covered, and refrigerated for up to 3 days.) Serve hot, sprinkled with additional parsley.

Turkey Soup

You may have a favorite family recipe for turkey soup. Here are some tips for making any turkey soup a little better.

To make broth from a large (16- to 26-pound) turkey, use 2 onions, 2 carrots, 2 celery ribs, 8 fresh parsley sprigs, $3/4$ teaspoon fresh thyme, and 2 small bay leaves with 6 to 8 quarts water, as needed, to cover the turkey in the pot.

Do not make broth from brined, marinated, or smoked turkey, as the auxiliary flavors can make for an oddly flavored broth and soup. If the turkey was glazed, rinse the clinging glaze from the skin, or discard the glazed skin.

Remove edible meat from the carcass before making the broth. Roasted meat clinging to the bone will retain little flavor after long simmering.

Breaking up the turkey carcass helps it fit into the pot better and releases flavor from the bones. The older and larger the turkey, the tougher the bones and connective tissues at the joints; a cleaver may come in handy. Otherwise, just separate the carcass as best you can at the joints. In any case, be careful, as the broken bones can be sharp.

Cook starchy ingredients such as rice and pasta separately, then add them to the soup. If added raw to simmering soup, they soak up too much of the liquid and make the soup too thick. Potatoes do not need precooking like rice and pasta, and can be used in soups without caveats.

Gravy and leftover stuffing with relatively neutral flavors can be used to enrich turkey soup. (Herbed white-bread stuffing works well, while oyster-cornbread stuffing would not.) As a flavor boost and to provide light thickening, stir gravy into the soup toward its finish. To thicken the soup, add 1 1/2 cups stuffing and let simmer for at least 30 minutes, stirring often, so the bread can "melt" into the soup.

Leftover turkey broth can be cooled, stored in an airtight container, and refrigerated for up to 3 days or frozen for up to 3 months. Turkey broth is an excellent all-purpose stock for both poultry and meat dishes.

If you want cream of turkey soup, it couldn't be easier. Just stir in as much (or as little) heavy cream as you dare. Usually, for a large pot of soup, I use about 1 cup. Don't use half-and-half, light cream, or milk, as they have lower butterfat contents, and may separate when they come into contact with the hot broth.

Celery Root
and Red Pepper Slaw

Here's a colorful fall slaw that is very versatile. It's easy to whip up for a weeknight meal, or use it as a first course for company, topped with grilled shrimp. The raw celery root will seem almost as firm as uncooked potatoes, but the soak in the vinaigrette softens it to a nice crunch.

1 ¼ pounds celery root (celeriac)

1 red bell pepper, cored and seeded, cut into thin strips

2 scallions, white and green parts, finely chopped

3 tablespoons sherry vinegar

1 teaspoon grainy mustard, such as moutarde de Meaux

1 teaspoon sugar

½ cup extra-virgin olive oil

Salt and freshly ground black pepper

1. Cut away the gnarly bottom of the celery root, then pare the entire root. Using a food processor fitted with the coarse shredding blade, shred the celery root. Transfer to a large bowl and add the bell pepper and scallions.

2. Combine the sherry vinegar, mustard, and sugar in a medium bowl. Gradually whisk in the olive oil. Season with salt and pepper. Pour over the vegetables and mix well. Cover and refrigerate for at least 1 hour to soften the celery root. (The slaw can be made up to 2 days ahead.) Serve chilled.

Pear, Pomegranate, and Greens Salad

Makes 6 servings

Two fruits that are indisputably at their best in autumn are pears and pomegranates, and they come together in this refreshing salad. To play up the ruby red theme, red-skinned Bartletts are especially good here. Sherry vinegar and bottled pomegranate juice make up the acidic components of the vinaigrette, but if your grocery store carries pomegranate balsamic vinegar, substitute it, if you wish.

POMEGRANATE VINAIGRETTE

1 ½ tablespoons sherry vinegar

2 tablespoons bottled pomegranate juice

¼ teaspoon salt

⅛ teaspoon freshly ground black pepper

⅓ cup vegetable oil

2 tablespoons imported walnut oil (see Note)

2 ripe pears, such as Anjou or Bartlett, cored and cut lengthwise into thin wedges

⅓ cup pomegranate seeds (see page 39)

⅓ cup walnuts, toasted and coarsely chopped (see Note, page 40)

5 ounces mixed baby greens, such as mesclun

Salt and freshly ground black pepper

1. To make the vinaigrette, whisk together the vinegar, pomegranate juice, salt, and pepper in a small bowl. Gradually whisk in the vegetable and walnut oils.

2.   Combine the pears, pomegranate seeds, and walnuts in a medium bowl. Add 2 tablespoons of the vinaigrette and mix gently.

3.   Toss the baby greens with the remaining vinaigrette in a large bowl. Add the pear mixture and toss again. Taste and adjust the seasoning with salt and pepper. Serve immediately.

Note

For the best results, be sure that the walnut oil is made from toasted walnuts. Most French nut oils, available at specialty food shops and many supermarkets, are prepared in this manner. Cold-pressed or expressed walnut oils aren't as flavorful.

Pomegranates

Pomegranates are often referred to as a "superfruit," being loaded with vitamin C and antioxidants. Culturally speaking, the pomegranate has always been a star, and it figures prominently in the Bible, Greek mythology, and other literary masterpieces. And Middle Eastern cuisine wouldn't be the same without it.

Open a pomegranate, and you will see clusters of red, juice-filled capsules. Officially, these are called *arils*, as the seeds are inside, but let's use the vernacular and call them seeds. The white membrane surrounding the clusters is bitter, so you need to free the seeds/arils. Of course, the easiest way to do this is with your teeth. But be prepared for the squirting, staining juice . . . which is part of the fun of eating them. And this won't work if you want to use the pomegranate seeds in a salad.

If you want to save your clothing, you can release the seeds from the membranes and eat them by the handful. Score the pomegranate lengthwise into quarters, just cutting into the thick skin, but not the seeds. Fill a large bowl with cold water. Submerge the entire pomegranate under the water. Gently break open the fruit, then coax the seeds away from the membranes. The seeds will sink to the bottom of the bowl, and the membrane will float on the water. Skim off the membranes, drain the seeds, and dig in.

Yes, you can squeeze the seeds to extract the juice. But bottled pomegranate juice is such a great product, and so convenient, that you can skip juicing.

Carrot, Cranberry, and Walnut Salad

Makes 4 to 6 servings

For a change of pace from leafy green salad, make this simple slaw for a weekend dinner. Toasting walnuts enhances their flavor, but you should use them untoasted rather than not making this delicious, colorful salad at all.

1 pound carrots

½ cup dried cranberries

½ cup toasted and coarsely chopped walnuts (see Note)

One 4-inch-long piece fresh ginger, peeled and shredded on a box grater

2 tablespoons minced shallot

2 tablespoons cider vinegar

⅓ cup vegetable oil

Salt and freshly ground black pepper

1. Using a food processor fitted with the coarse shredding blade, shred the carrots. Combine the carrots, cranberries, and walnuts in a large bowl.

2. A handful at a time, squeeze the shredded ginger into a medium bowl to extract the juice. You should have 2 tablespoons ginger juice. Add the shallot and vinegar. Gradually whisk in the oil. Pour over the carrot mixture and mix well. Cover and refrigerate to soften the cranberries, about 1 hour. (The salad can be made up to 2 days ahead.) Season with salt and pepper to taste. Serve chilled.

Note

To toast walnuts, preheat the oven to 350°F. Spread the walnuts on a baking sheet. Bake, stirring often, until lightly toasted and fragrant, about 10 minutes. Cool completely.

Cauliflower Salad with Parsley-Caper Vinaigrette

Makes 8 servings

This simple but vibrantly flavored salad makes a nice first course to a simple roasted main course such as the Roasted Loin of Pork with Brussels Sprouts on page 80. Don't leave out the anchovy—it adds an elusive saltiness to the vinaigrette that won't be overly fishy.

1 head cauliflower, about 1 pound, 14 ounces

2 tablespoons red wine vinegar

½ teaspoon anchovy paste

1 garlic clove, crushed through a press

½ cup extra-virgin olive oil

3 tablespoons bottled nonpareil capers, drained and rinsed

3 tablespoons finely chopped fresh parsley

Salt and freshly ground black pepper

1. Bring a large pot of lightly salted water to a boil over high heat. Trim the cauliflower and cut it into bite-size florets. Add to the water and cook until crisp-tender, about 5 minutes. Drain and rinse under cold running water until cool. Drain well. Spread the cauliflower on paper towels, cover with more paper towels, and let cool completely.

2. Whisk together the vinegar, anchovy paste, and garlic in a medium bowl. Whisk in the oil. Stir in the capers and parsley. Season with salt and pepper to taste.

3. Add the cauliflower to the vinaigrette and toss. Cover and refrigerate for at least 1 hour and up to 8 hours before serving. Serve chilled or at room temperature.

MAIN COURSES

Dry-Brined Roasted Turkey with Sage and Cider Gravy

Red-Eye Chili

Tailgate Hoboken Cheesesteaks

Leg of Lamb with Roasted Ratatouille

Lamb Tagine in Roasted Whole Pumpkin

Chicken Pot Pie "au Vin"

Roasted Chicken Breasts with Root Vegetables and Thyme

Asian-Braised Duck Legs with Chestnuts and Carrots

Pork Pot Roast with Dried Figs and Herbs

Crab-Stuffed Portobello Mushrooms

Roasted Salmon with Pomegranate Butter Sauce

Roasted Loin of Pork with Brussels Sprouts

Oktoberfest Sausages and Red Cabbage

Dry-Brined Roasted Turkey with Sage and Cider Gravy

Makes about 16 servings with about 6 cups gravy

Make-Ahead: Salt and refrigerate the turkey the day before roasting

While I am perfectly happy with the simple roasted turkey that I have been teaching for years (cover the breast with foil and kiss worries about dry white meat good-bye), I do want to acknowledge other cooking methods. Salting the bird a day ahead does a nice job of seasoning the turkey without overwhelming it with unnecessary flavors. This amount of salt and herbs works for a 16- to 18-pound bird, but it can be adjusted a tablespoon or two in either direction for larger or smaller birds; it is better to under-salt slightly than to oversalt. Dry-brining only works with fresh, "all natural" turkeys. Do not use any turkey that has been injected with sodium solutions (frozen turkeys are always processed this way), or the bird will end up too salty. This recipe may seem long, but believe me, it is easy, and it's only lengthy because I've provided details to be sure that your holiday bird will be the best it can possibly be.

One 16- to 18-pound fresh turkey

TURKEY STOCK

1 tablespoon vegetable oil

1 small onion, chopped

1 small celery rib, chopped

1 small carrot, chopped

2 large turkey wings (about 1 pound each), chopped between the joints (optional)

2 quarts canned low-sodium chicken broth

4 parsley sprigs

¼ teaspoon dried thyme

¼ teaspoon dried peppercorns

1 bay leaf

DRY BRINE RUB

6 tablespoons kosher salt

1 ¼ teaspoons dried thyme

1 ¼ teaspoons dried rubbed sage

1 ¼ teaspoons crumbled dried rosemary

1 ¼ teaspoons dried marjoram

1 teaspoon freshly ground black pepper

2 bay leaves, well crumbled

Cornbread Stuffing with Dried Fruits and Hazelnuts (page 108), Italian-Style Stuffing with
    Sausage, Fennel, and Mushrooms (page 110), or about 10 cups of your favorite stuffing

8 tablespoons (1 stick) unsalted butter, at room temperature, plus more if needed

Salt and freshly ground black pepper

¾ cup all-purpose flour

½ cup hard apple cider (see Note, page 86)

1 tablespoon finely chopped fresh sage

1. The day before roasting the turkey, remove the neck and giblets from the turkey. Using a heavy knife or a cleaver, chop the neck into 2-inch chunks. Discard the liver, or save for another use. Pull out the yellow fat pads on either side of the tail (some producers remove these), cover, and refrigerate. Set the turkey aside.

2. To make the turkey stock, heat the oil in a large soup pot over medium-high heat. Add the turkey neck and giblets and cook, turning occasionally, until well browned,

about 10 minutes. Add the onion, celery, and carrot and cook, stirring occasionally, until the onion softens, about 5 minutes. If using the wings, add them to the pot at this point, but no need to brown them. Add the broth and enough cold water to cover the turkey parts by 1 inch. Bring to a boil over high heat, skimming off any foam that rises to the surface. Add the parsley, thyme, peppercorns, and bay leaf. Reduce the heat to low. Simmer, uncovered, until the stock is full-flavored, about 3 hours. Strain through a wire sieve into a bowl. You should have about 2 ½ quarts broth; add more chicken broth or water, if necessary. Cool completely. Cover and refrigerate overnight.

3. To make the dry brine rub, mix the salt, thyme, sage, rosemary, marjoram, ground pepper, and bay leaves in a small bowl. Rinse the turkey inside and out, but do not pat dry. Place the turkey in a turkey-size oven roasting bag. Sprinkle the dry brine inside and on the outside of the bird, coating it evenly. Close the bag and refrigerate for 18 to 24 hours.

4. The next day, position a rack in the lowest position of the oven and preheat to 325°F. Scrape off and discard the solidified fat on the surface of the stock. Transfer the stock to a large saucepan and bring to a boil over medium heat. Remove the stock from the heat.

5. Remove the turkey from the bag and rinse thoroughly under cold water. Pat the turkey skin dry. Turn the turkey on its breast. Loosely fill the neck cavity with stuffing (or with the chopped vegetable mixture; see Variation). Using a thin wooden or metal skewer, pin the turkey's neck skin to the back. Fold the turkey's wings akimbo behind the back or tie to the body with kitchen string. Turn the turkey over. Loosely fill the large body cavity with stuffing. Place any remaining stuffing in a lightly buttered casserole, cover, and refrigerate to bake later as a side dish. Place the drumsticks in the hock lock (the metal or plastic implement that some producers insert in the tail area) or tie together with kitchen string.

Turkey Talk

Turkey is an enormous subject; I have written two books about it. Here are a few tips to guarantee a great holiday bird on your table.

- A fresh turkey has the most natural flavor. The easiest rule of thumb for serving portions is to estimate 1 pound of uncooked turkey per person, as the bones can make up a fair amount of the weight. There's no difference in flavor between a hen and a tom, so just buy a turkey of the size you need.

- Use a high-quality roasting pan, which will absorb the oven heat and help create dark, rich drippings that in turn make great gravy.

- An accurate meat thermometer is a must. Don't trust the pop-up thermometers that come with some turkeys as they often get glued shut by the roasting juices. My favorite thermometer is the digital probe thermometer with the readout that sits outside of the stove, which indicates the temperature without requiring that you open the door.

- Basting does not keep the bird moist, but it does help create a gorgeous browned skin. Don't overdo basting, as every time the oven door is opened, the temperature will drop.

- Be sure to let the roasted turkey stand at room temperature for at least 30 minutes before carving to allow the hot juices in the bird to redistribute themselves. This also gives you a good-size window for heating side dishes and making gravy.

- Do not bother to tent the bird with foil. This only allows steam to gather, which will soften the skin.

6. Place the turkey, breast side up, on a rack in the roasting pan. Rub all over with the softened butter. Season with salt and pepper. Tightly cover the breast area with aluminum foil. Pour 2 cups of the turkey stock into the bottom of the pan. Add the reserved turkey fat to the pan.

7. Roast the turkey, basting all over every 45 minutes or so with the juices on the bottom of the pan (lift up the foil to reach the breast area), until a meat thermometer inserted in the meaty part of the thigh (but not touching a bone) reads 180°F and the stuffing is at least 160°F, about 4 hours. (See Estimated Roasting Times, page 51.) Whenever the drippings evaporate to a brown glaze, add stock or water to moisten them (about 1 cup at a time). During the last hour, remove the foil and baste a couple of times with the pan juices.

8. Transfer the turkey to a large serving platter and let it stand for at least 30 minutes before carving. Increase the oven temperature to 350°F. Drizzle ½ cup of the turkey stock over the stuffing in the casserole, cover, and bake until heated through, about 30 minutes.

9. Meanwhile, pour the drippings from the roasting pan into a heat-proof glass bowl or measuring cup. Let stand for 5 minutes; then skim off and reserve the clear yellow fat that rises to the top. Measure 9 tablespoons fat, into a small bowl, adding melted butter if needed. Add enough turkey stock to the skimmed drippings to make 6 cups total.

10. Place the roasting pan over two stove burners on low heat and add the 9 tablespoons of turkey fat. Whisk in the flour, scraping up the browned bits on the bottom of the pan, and cook until lightly browned, about 2 minutes. Whisk in the cider, and then the stock mixture. Bring to a boil, then reduce the heat to medium-low. Simmer, whisking often, until the gravy has thickened and no trace of raw flour flavor remains, about

5 minutes. Strain into a clean 2-quart measuring cup. Season the gravy with salt and pepper, then stir in the sage. Pour into a warmed gravy boat. Carve the turkey and serve the stuffing and gravy alongside.

Variation

Not everyone likes to stuff turkey, and an unstuffed bird does roast more quickly than a stuffed one. If you prefer, stuff the bird with vegetables and herbs to flavor the meat and juices, but these will not be served as a side dish. Mix 1 onion, 1 celery rib, and 1 carrot, chopped, with 2 tablespoons chopped fresh parsley and 1 teaspoon each dried rosemary, thyme, sage, and marjoram. Use the vegetable mixture to stuff the neck and body cavities. After roasting the turkey, tilt it so the tasty juices run out of the body cavity into the roasting pan to add flavor to the gravy.

A Thanksgiving Menu

Butternut Squash Bisque with Chipotle–Red Pepper Swirl (page 23)

Dry-Brined Roasted Turkey with Sage and Cider Gravy (page 44)

Cornbread Stuffing with Dried Fruits and Hazelnuts (page 108)

Mashed Potatoes with Mascarpone and Roasted Garlic (page 119)

Roasted Yams with Orange-Chipotle Glaze (page 120)

Green Beans with Caramelized Shallot Butter (page 118)

Cranberry Rum-Raisin Sauce (page 124)

Pumpkin Hazelnut Bars (page 151)

Estimated Roasting Times

(Oven Temperature: 325°F)

Add an extra 30 minutes to the roasting time to allow for variations in roasting conditions. It's better to have the turkey done ahead of time than to keep everyone hungry and waiting for the bird to finish roasting.

UNSTUFFED TURKEY

8 TO 12 POUNDS	$2\frac{3}{4}$ TO 3 HOURS
12 TO 14 POUNDS	3 TO $3\frac{3}{4}$ HOURS
14 TO 18 POUNDS	$3\frac{3}{4}$ TO $4\frac{1}{4}$ HOURS
18 TO 20 POUNDS	$4\frac{1}{4}$ TO $4\frac{1}{2}$ HOURS
20 TO 24 POUNDS	$4\frac{1}{2}$ TO 5 HOURS

STUFFED TURKEY

8 TO 12 POUNDS	3 TO $3\frac{1}{2}$ HOURS
12 TO 14 POUNDS	$3\frac{1}{2}$ TO 4 HOURS
14 TO 18 POUNDS	4 TO $4\frac{1}{4}$ HOURS
18 TO 20 POUNDS	$4\frac{1}{4}$ TO $4\frac{3}{4}$ HOURS
20 TO 24 POUNDS	$4\frac{3}{4}$ TO $5\frac{1}{4}$ HOURS

Red-Eye Chili

Chili just might be the ultimate autumn dish: it will add warmth to a cool evening and it can heat up the chilliest tailgate cookout (no pun intended). The deep flavor of coffee complements the beef, and a bit of chocolate balances the spicy sauce. Pure ancho chile powder can be found in Latino markets and in the spice section of many supermarkets. It has sweet and spicy notes, and regular chili powder is not a good substitute, as its flavor is harsher. The chili is great just as it is, but add your favorite toppings (sour cream, Cheddar cheese, chopped onions or scallions, and the like) if you're in the mood.

2 tablespoons extra-virgin olive oil, or more as needed

3 pounds boneless beef chuck, cut into 1-inch cubes

1 teaspoon salt, plus more to taste

½ teaspoon freshly ground black pepper, plus more to taste

1 large onion, chopped

1 large red bell pepper, seeded, cored, and chopped

1 jalapeño pepper, seeds and ribs discarded, finely chopped

6 garlic cloves, finely chopped

2 tablespoons pure ground ancho chile

1 tablespoon dried oregano

1 tablespoon ground cumin

2 cups strong brewed coffee (not dark-roast or espresso)

One 14½-ounce can diced tomatoes in juice, drained

¼ cup yellow cornmeal

1 ounce unsweetened chocolate, coarsely chopped

1. Position a rack in the center of the oven and preheat the oven to 300°F.

2. In a large Dutch oven, heat 1 tablespoon of the oil over medium-high heat. Season the beef with the salt and pepper. In batches without crowding, add the beef and cook, turning occasionally and adding more oil as needed, until browned, about 8 minutes. Using a slotted spoon, transfer the beef to a plate.

3. Pour out all but 2 tablespoons of fat from the pot and return the pot to medium heat. Add the onion, bell pepper, and jalapeño and cook, stirring often, until tender, about 6 minutes. Stir in the garlic and cook until fragrant, about 1 minute. Stir in the ground ancho chile, oregano, and cumin and stir for 15 seconds. Stir in the coffee and tomatoes. Bring to a boil over high heat, scraping up the browned bits in the pan. Return the beef and any collected juices to the pot.

4. Cover the pot and place in the oven. Bake until the meat is very tender, about 2¼ hours.

5. Remove from the oven and let stand for 5 minutes. Skim off and discard the fat that rises to the surface. Return the pot to medium heat. Whisk in the cornmeal and chocolate. Cook until the sauce boils and thickens, about 2 minutes. Season with salt and pepper. Serve hot.

Tailgate Hoboken Cheesesteaks

Makes 6 sandwiches

When I lived near Hoboken, New Jersey, I frequented Piccolo's, a place that was right out of *The Sopranos*. (If you doubt me, you should know that there was once a famous sting here that involved microphones hidden in the jukeboxes . . . which only play Sinatra.) This restaurant is famous for its cheesesteaks, which are made with thin top loin beef steaks and not the shaved beef that many Philadelphia joints serve. Serve these at a tailgate, and you will be more popular than the winning quarterback. The instructions assume that these will be cooked in a charcoal grill, but the recipe can be adjusted to a gas grill.

2 large onions, thinly sliced

4 garlic cloves, thinly sliced

2 tablespoons extra-virgin olive oil

Salt and freshly ground black pepper

2 large red bell peppers, seeded, cored, and thinly sliced

6 top loin (also called shell, strip, or New York) beef steaks, cut ¼ inch thick (see Note)

12 thin slices mozzarella cheese, trimmed to fit the steaks

6 crusty rolls, about 6 inches long, split open

1. Toss the onions and garlic in a bowl with 1 tablespoon of the oil, ½ teaspoon salt, and ½ teaspoon pepper. Wrap in a packet of heavy-duty aluminum foil. Repeat with the bell peppers, 1 tablespoon oil, ½ teaspoon salt, and ¼ teaspoon pepper, and wrap them in another foil packet.

2. Season the steaks with 1½ teaspoons salt and ½ teaspoon pepper. Place in a zippered plastic bag. (The onions, peppers, and steaks can be prepared and refrigerated up to 1 day ahead. If cooking at a tailgate, transport them in an ice chest to the event.)

3. Build a fire in a charcoal grill and let burn just until the coals are covered with white ash. Leave the coals heaped in the center and do not spread them out. Place the packets of vegetables on the cooler perimeter of the grill and cover. Cook, occasionally turning the packets with tongs, until the vegetables are tender (open a packet to check), about 30 minutes. Remove from the heat.

4. Add about 16 fresh briquettes to the grill and let them burn until covered with white ash. Spread the coals out in the grill. Lightly oil the grill grate. Place the steaks on the grill and cover. Grill, turning once, until the underside is seared with grill marks, about 2 minutes. Turn and grill the other side, about 2 minutes for medium-rare meat. Just before removing the steaks from the grill, top each steak with 2 mozzarella slices. Transfer to a carving board.

5. Add the rolls to the grill, cut sides down, and toast them. Open the vegetable packets. If necessary, cut each steak in half to fit in the rolls. Place a steak in each roll, and top with the onion-garlic mixture and the peppers. Serve hot.

Note

If the butcher doesn't cooperate by providing the thin-sliced steaks, you can slice your own. Purchase a 2-pound top loin roast. Wrap the roast in aluminum foil and freeze just until partially frozen, about 2 hours. Using a sharp carving knife, slice the roast crosswise into ¼-inch-thick slices.

Tailgating Menu

White Bean Dip with Roasted Garlic (page 16)

Tailgate Hoboken Cheesesteaks (page 55)

Cauliflower Salad with Parsley-Caper Vinaigrette (page 41)

Fig Bars (page 131)

Leg of Lamb with Roasted Ratatouille

Makes 6 servings

While late-season summer vegetables such as eggplant, zucchini, and tomatoes may not be as full-flavored as the vegetables at their peak, cooked together they combine to make a great ratatouille, especially when cooked with the lamb to pick up its meaty juices. Serve this fragrant entrée with orzo, tossed with olive oil and grated aged goat's cheese.

GARLIC OIL

5 tablespoons extra-virgin olive oil

3 large garlic cloves, crushed under a knife

RATATOUILLE

1 medium eggplant, cut into 1-inch chunks

1 ½ teaspoons salt

6 ripe plum tomatoes, halved lengthwise, seeded, and cut into 1-inch chunks

1 large zucchini, cut lengthwise, then into 1-inch lengths

1 large red bell pepper, seeded, cored, and cut into 1-inch pieces

1 large onion, cut into 1-inch chunks

1 ½ teaspoons herbes de Provence

½ teaspoon crushed hot red pepper

LAMB

One 2 ¾-pound boneless leg of lamb, trimmed and butterflied

1 ½ teaspoons salt

½ teaspoon freshly ground black pepper

2 teaspoons herbes de Provence

1. To make the garlic oil, heat the oil and garlic in a small saucepan over low heat until bubbles form around the garlic. Remove from the heat and let stand for 1 hour. Remove and discard the garlic.

2. Meanwhile, prepare the ratatouille. Toss the eggplant with the salt in a large colander. Let stand for 1 hour in the sink. Rinse the eggplant well under cold running water. Drain and pat the eggplant dry with paper towels.

3. Preheat the oven to 400°F. Toss the eggplant, tomatoes, zucchini, bell pepper, onion, herbes de Provence, and crushed red pepper with 3 tablespoons of the garlic oil. Spread in a large roasting pan. Roast for 40 minutes.

4. Meanwhile, to prepare the lamb, brush the lamb on both sides with the remaining 2 tablespoons garlic oil. Season with the salt and pepper. Sprinkle the smooth side of the lamb with the herbes de Provence. Let stand at room temperature while the ratatouille roasts.

5. Stir the ratatouille well. Place the lamb on top of the ratatouille. Roast until an instant-read thermometer inserted in the thickest part of the lamb reads 130°F (for medium-rare lamb), 30 to 35 minutes.

6. Transfer the lamb to a carving board and let stand for 5 minutes. Transfer the ratatouille to a serving platter. Carve the lamb, arrange the slices over the ratatouille, and serve.

Lamb Tagine in Roasted Whole Pumpkin

Makes 6 to 8 servings

This beautifully spiced Moroccan lamb stew stands on its own. But, for a show-stopping presentation, serve it in a whole pumpkin. Look for a cooking pumpkin, which is smaller and has a thicker shell and tastier flesh than the jack-o'-lantern variety. Once you learn how to roast a whole pumpkin, you may use it as an edible bowl for other stews—chili, for example. As for the tagine, take care not to overcook the lean leg of lamb. It will not be stewed as long as tougher cuts.

ROASTED PUMPKIN

One 4-pound cooking pumpkin, such as sugar or cheese pumpkin

½ teaspoon salt

¼ teaspoon freshly ground black pepper

LAMB TAGINE

4 tablespoons extra-virgin olive oil, divided

1½ pounds boneless leg of lamb, well trimmed, cut into 1-inch pieces

½ teaspoon salt, plus more to taste

½ teaspoon freshly ground black pepper, plus more to taste

2 cups canned low-sodium chicken broth

1 teaspoon harissa (see Note), or more to taste

1 large onion, chopped

2 carrots, cut into ¼-inch-thick rounds

2 garlic cloves, finely chopped

1 teaspoon ground ginger

½ teaspoon ground cinnamon

¼ teaspoon crushed hot red pepper

One 28-ounce can diced tomatoes, drained

One 15- to 19-ounce can garbanzo beans (chickpeas), drained and rinsed

Hot cooked couscous, for serving

1. Position a rack in the lower third of the oven and preheat the oven to 400°F. Lightly oil a rimmed baking sheet.

2. To roast the pumpkin, using a sturdy paring knife, cut into the pumpkin top around the stem to create a lid about 6 inches in diameter. Lift off the lid and set aside. Using a large metal spoon, scrape out the fibers and seeds from inside the pumpkin and discard them. (If you wish, remove the seeds from the fibers and reserve the seeds for roasting.) Season the inside of the pumpkin shell and lid with the salt and pepper. Return the lid to the pumpkin and place the pumpkin on the baking sheet. Bake until the inside of the pumpkin is tender when the interior flesh is scraped with a spoon (remove the lid to check), about 1¼ hours.

3. Meanwhile, make the tagine. Heat 2 tablespoons of the oil in a large Dutch oven over medium-high heat. Season the lamb with ½ teaspoon salt and ½ teaspoon pepper. In batches, add to the pot and cook, stirring occasionally, until lightly browned, about 4 minutes. (The lamb should be rare at this point.) Using a slotted spoon, transfer the lamb to a plate.

4. Add the broth to the pot and bring to a boil, stirring to release the browned bits in the bottom of the pot. Pour the broth into a large glass measuring cup or heat-proof bowl. Transfer ½ cup of the broth to a sauceboat or small bowl and stir in the harissa

to make a very spicy seasoning sauce for the finished tagine. Set the harissa sauce aside. Reserve the remaining broth.

5. Add the remaining 2 tablespoons oil to the pot and heat over medium heat. Add the onion and carrots and cook, stirring occasionally, until the onion is golden, about 6 minutes. Stir in the garlic and cook until fragrant, about 1 minute. Stir in the ginger, cinnamon, and crushed hot pepper and cook for 15 seconds. Stir in the tomatoes, then the reserved chicken broth, and bring to a boil. Reduce the heat to low, cover, and simmer until the carrots are tender, about 20 minutes. Return the lamb and any collected juices to the pot, and stir in the garbanzo beans. Increase the heat to medium-high and cook just until the beans are heated through, about 5 minutes. Season with salt and pepper to taste.

6. To serve, carefully transfer the roasted pumpkin to a serving platter. Remove the lid, ladle in the tagine, and replace the lid. (Do not worry if all of the tagine won't fit into the pumpkin; just reserve it in a serving bowl.) Present the pumpkin at the table. Spoon the tagine onto individual plates. When the tagine is served and the pumpkin is empty, cut the pumpkin into wedges and add to the plates. Serve the tagine and pumpkin wedges immediately, with the couscous and harissa sauce passed on the side.

Note

Harissa is a very hot chile paste available at Middle Eastern and Mediterranean grocers. To store it, transfer the harissa from its can to a small covered jar and refrigerate for up to 2 months. If you can't find harissa, substitute Chinese chili paste with garlic, or even Tabasco.

Pumpkins for Cooking

Quite a bit smaller than carving pumpkins, cooking pumpkins usually don't weigh more than three pounds. Look for varieties with names like Sugar, Cheese, or Pie, which have thick walls that yield lots of savory flesh. Baking is the best way to cook them, as steaming makes them soggy.

Solid-pack canned pumpkin is a reliable product and a great timesaver. However, when I have the time, I do roast pumpkin flesh to puree for baked goods. You will get about one cup of puree for every pound of pumpkin, but always buy more than you think you need to allow for variables.

Cut off the stem, then cut the pumpkin in half vertically and scoop out the seeds. Place the unpeeled pumpkin halves,

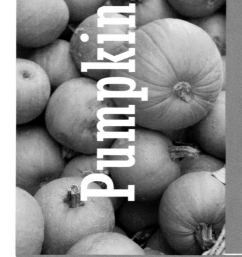

cut sides down, in a foil-lined baking pan, and add 1 cup hot tap water. Cover loosely with foil and bake in a preheated 350°F oven until the pumpkin is easily pierced with the tip of a knife, about 45 minutes, depending on the density of the pumpkin. Remove from the pan and cool until easy to handle. Scoop the flesh from the skin, and process in a food processor or blender until smooth. The consistency should be like heavy-bodied applesauce, and it should be thick enough to support a standing wooden spoon. If the pumpkin puree is too thin, simmer it in a saucepan over low heat, stirring often, until the excess liquid is evaporated and the puree is thickened.

Chicken Pot Pie "au Vin"

Makes 6 servings

Chicken pot pie, in most of its American incarnations, is a home-style dish that exemplifies the best of farmhouse cooking. For an earthier dish with the more robust flavors of mushrooms, pancetta, and red wine, try this version. Substitute thawed frozen puff pastry for the homemade pastry dough, if you wish.

Flour for rolling out the dough

Perfect Butter Pastry Dough (page 140)

2 teaspoons vegetable oil

2 ounces pancetta or rindless slab bacon, cut into ¼-inch dice

2 pounds boneless and skinless chicken thighs, cut into 1-inch pieces

½ teaspoon salt, plus more to taste

¼ teaspoon freshly ground black pepper, plus more to taste

2 tablespoons unsalted butter

10 ounces cremini or white mushrooms, cut into quarters

2 carrots, cut into ½-inch dice

⅓ cup finely chopped shallots

1 garlic clove, minced

3 tablespoons all-purpose flour

1 cup hearty red wine, such as Syrah-Cabernet blend

2 cups canned low-sodium chicken broth

2 teaspoons tomato paste

¾ teaspoon dried thyme

¾ teaspoon dried rosemary

1. Position a rack in the top third of the oven and preheat the oven to 375°F. Set aside a 13 x 9-inch rectangular baking dish.

2. On a lightly floured work surface, roll out the dough into a 13 x 9-inch rectangle about $\frac{1}{8}$ inch thick. Slide onto a rimless baking sheet and refrigerate while making the filling.

3. Heat the oil in a large skillet over medium heat. Add the pancetta and cook, stirring occasionally, until browned, about 10 minutes. Using a slotted spoon, transfer to a plate, leaving the fat in the pan. Increase the heat to medium-high.

4. Season the chicken thighs with $\frac{1}{2}$ teaspoon salt and $\frac{1}{4}$ teaspoon pepper. In batches without crowding, add to the skillet and cook, stirring occasionally, until lightly browned, about 5 minutes. Transfer to the plate.

5. Melt the butter in the skillet. Add the mushrooms and cook, stirring often, until they begin to brown, about 10 minutes. Stir in the carrots, shallots, and garlic and cook until the shallots soften, about 2 minutes. Sprinkle with the flour and stir well. Stir in the red wine, then the broth, tomato paste, thyme, and rosemary. Bring to a simmer. Stir in the reserved pancetta and chicken. Season with salt and pepper.

6. Pour the mixture into the baking dish. Trim the chilled pastry to fit just inside of the baking dish and cut a couple of slits in the pastry. Slide the pastry into the dish to cover the filling. Bake until the crust is golden brown and the sauce is bubbling, about 30 minutes. Let stand for 5 minutes, then serve hot.

Roasted Chicken Breasts with Root Vegetables and Thyme

Makes 4 servings

The secret to juicy chicken with burnished golden brown skin? Roast it at a relatively high temperature, and do not overcook it. Be forewarned that you will have more smoke than when you roast at lower temperatures, but the results are worth it. Cook some root vegetables in the same pan with the breasts for a one-pan meal.

2 tablespoons extra-virgin olive oil, plus more for the pan

4 medium red-skinned potatoes, scrubbed and cut into 1-inch pieces

2 medium carrots, peeled and cut into 1-inch pieces

1 medium turnip, peeled and cut into 1-inch pieces

1 medium parsnip, peeled and cut into 1-inch pieces

2 teaspoons chopped fresh thyme, divided

1½ teaspoons salt, divided

1 teaspoon freshly ground black pepper, divided

4 chicken breasts halves with skin and bone, about 10 ounces each

1 cup canned low-sodium chicken broth

1 tablespoon unsalted butter, chilled

1. Position a rack in the upper third of the oven and preheat the oven to 425°F. Lightly oil a roasting pan.

2. Toss the potatoes, carrots, turnip, and parsnip in a large bowl with the oil, 1 teaspoon of the thyme, ¾ teaspoon of the salt, and ½ teaspoon of the pepper. Spread in the

roasting pan. Season the chicken with the remaining ¾ teaspoon salt and ½ teaspoon pepper, then sprinkle with the remaining 1 teaspoon thyme. Nestle the chicken, skin side up, among the vegetables.

3. Roast, occasionally scraping up and turning the vegetables with a metal spatula, until the vegetables are tender and an instant-read thermometer inserted in the thickest part of the chicken breasts reads 170°F, about 35 minutes. Transfer the chicken and vegetables to a platter. If the chicken is tender before the vegetables are done, tent the chicken with foil, then continue roasting the vegetables. In either case, tent the platter while making the pan sauce.

4. Place the roasting pan over 2 burners on high heat. Add the broth and bring to a boil, scraping up the browned bits in the bottom and sides of the pan. Boil until reduced to about ⅓ cup, about 5 minutes. Remove from the heat, and whisk in the butter to lightly thicken the sauce. Pour over the chicken and vegetables and serve hot.

Asian-Braised Duck Legs with Chestnuts and Carrots

Duck is another food that seems happiest when served during cool weather. Duck legs have succulent meat that braises beautifully and pairs well with the bold flavors of ginger and chestnuts. They are easy to find at Asian markets, but many supermarkets carry them now, as well. Serve this over rice to get every last bit of the sauce.

2 tablespoons vegetable oil

4 duck leg quarters

½ teaspoon salt

½ teaspoon freshly ground black pepper

2 scallions, white and green parts, chopped

1 tablespoon peeled and minced fresh ginger

2 cups canned low-sodium chicken broth

½ cup soy sauce

⅓ cup dry sherry

3 tablespoons light brown sugar

2 star anise pods

¼ teaspoon crushed hot red pepper

6 ounces baby-cut carrots

1 cup vacuum-packed chestnuts

1 tablespoon cornstarch dissolved in 3 tablespoons water

Hot cooked rice, for serving

1. Heat the oil in a Dutch oven over medium-high heat. Season the duck with the salt and pepper. In batches, add to the Dutch oven, skin sides down, and cook, turning occasionally, until browned, about 5 minutes. Transfer to a plate. Pour off all but 2 tablespoons of fat from the pot.

2. Add the scallions and ginger and stir until the ginger is fragrant, about 30 seconds. Stir in the broth, soy sauce, sherry, brown sugar, star anise, and hot red pepper. Bring to a boil and return the duck to the pot. Cover and reduce the heat to medium-low. Simmer for 40 minutes.

3. Add the baby carrots to the pot. Simmer until the duck and carrots are tender, about 20 minutes. During the last 5 minutes, stir in the chestnuts. Using a slotted spoon, transfer the duck, carrots, and chestnuts to a deep serving bowl.

4. Strain the cooking liquid into a large fat separator. Let stand for 5 minutes, then pour the degreased cooking liquid back into the pot, leaving the fat in the separator. (You can also skim the fat from the cooking liquid in the pot with a large spoon.) Bring to a boil over high heat. Whisk in the cornstarch mixture and cook until the liquid thickens, about 15 seconds. Pour over the duck mixture in the serving bowl. Serve hot with the rice.

Chestnuts

For many families, it isn't Thanksgiving without chestnut stuffing. This must be based on a very old tradition, because chestnuts have not been a significant American crop since 1904, when a blight wiped out most of the chestnut trees in the country. Since then, American chestnut trees have been crossed with disease-resistant Asian trees.

Most chestnuts in the market have been imported from Europe or Asia. Frankly, by the time you buy them, they can be pretty old, and the ones that haven't outright rotted are very difficult to roast and peel. For my money, when I want fresh chestnuts, I order them from a small producer, such as www.buychestnuts.com or www.chestnutsforsale.com. Roasted, peeled, and vacuum-packed chestnuts, sold in jars or in plastic packs, are now available at specialty food stores, Asian grocers, and many supermarkets.

If you get fresh American chestnuts, they must be roasted and peeled before eating. Using a short, sturdy knife, such as a paring knife, cut a shallow X in the flat side of the nut, cutting just into the flesh. Spread on a baking sheet and bake in a pre-heated 400°F oven until the slashes have curled and the flesh is golden, about 30 minutes. Let the chestnuts cool for a few minutes, then peel them while they are still warm, removing both the thick outer peel and the thin brown inner skin.

Pork Pot Roast with Dried Figs and Herbs

Makes 8 to 10 servings

A long-simmered pot roast doesn't have to be made with beef, as this pork version illustrates. Made with a large pork butt, it feeds a crowd. Plan on making mashed potatoes to serve for soaking up the luscious sauce, made sweet with dried figs cooked along with the pork.

2 cups dry white wine, such as Pinot Grigio

7 ounces dried Calimyrna figs

1½ teaspoons salt, plus more to taste

1½ teaspoons dried rosemary

1½ teaspoons dried sage

½ teaspoon ground fennel seed (grind in a spice grinder or in a mortar and pestle)

¾ teaspoon freshly ground black pepper, plus more to taste

One 7-pound pork butt with bone, skin trimmed

2 tablespoons extra-virgin olive oil, as needed

1 large onion, chopped

3 medium carrots, chopped

2 tablespoons unsalted butter, at room temperature

2 tablespoons all-purpose flour

1. Bring the wine to a simmer in a small nonreactive saucepan over high heat. Remove from the heat and add the figs. Let stand until cooled, about 1 hour.

2. Mix together the 1½ teaspoons salt, the rosemary, sage, fennel seed, and ¾ teaspoon pepper. Using the tip of a knife, poke about a dozen slits in the pork. Rub the herb mixture all over the pork, forcing some of the mixture into the slits. Heat the oil in a large Dutch oven over medium-high heat. Add the pork and cook, turning occasionally, until browned, about 10 minutes. Transfer to a platter.

3. Add more oil to the pot, if needed. Add the onion and carrots and cook, stirring occasionally, until the onion softens, about 5 minutes. Return the pork to the pot, and add the figs and their wine. Bring to a boil over high heat. Reduce the heat to low and cover. Simmer until the pork is fork-tender, about 4 hours. Transfer the pork to a deep serving platter. Using a slotted spoon, transfer about half of the figs to the platter. Cover with aluminum foil to keep warm.

4. Remove the pot from the heat and let stand for 5 minutes. Using a large spoon, skim off and discard the fat that rises to the surface of the cooking liquid. Using a rubber spatula, mash the butter and flour together into a paste in a medium bowl. In batches, in a blender with the lid vented, puree the cooking liquid with the onions, carrots, and remaining figs. Whisk each batch of puree into the flour paste. Pour the pureed mixture back into the pot and bring to a boil over high heat, whisking often. Reduce the heat to medium-low and simmer until the sauce has thickened nicely, about 5 minutes. Season with salt and pepper.

5. Carve the pork. Pour the sauce over the pork and serve hot, with the figs.

Crab-Stuffed Portobello Mushrooms

If you have ever had small crab-stuffed mushrooms as finger food at a party, then you know how popular they are. Turned into a meal-size main course, perhaps served with Celery Root and Red Pepper Slaw (page 35), they make a good argument for Mae West's line, "Too much of a good thing can be wonderful."

CRAB FILLING

1 pound crabmeat, picked over for shells and cartilage

1 large egg, beaten

½ cup panko (Japanese bread crumbs)

¼ cup mayonnaise

¼ cup finely chopped scallions

1 teaspoon Worcestershire sauce

1 teaspoon Old Bay seasoning

¼ teaspoon salt

¼ teaspoon hot red pepper sauce

6 portobello mushrooms, about 3½ inches in diameter

6 tablespoons panko, for topping

Olive oil, for drizzling

Chopped fresh parsley, for serving

Lemon wedges, for serving

1. Position a rack in the top third of the oven and preheat to 400°F. Lightly oil a baking sheet.

2. To make the crab filling, mix together the crab, egg, panko, mayonnaise, scallions, Worcestershire sauce, Old Bay seasoning, salt, and hot pepper sauce until combined. Cover and refrigerate until ready to use, up to 2 hours.

3. Trim the mushroom stems flush with the caps; discard the stems, or save for another use. Rinse the mushrooms quickly under cold running water to remove any grit. Using the tip of a spoon, scrape out the dark gills from the undersides of the caps. Fill each mushroom cap with the crab mixture, mounding the filling in the cap. Place the caps, filling sides up, on the baking sheet. Sprinkle the filling in each cap with 1 tablespoon of panko and drizzle with oil.

4. Bake until the panko is golden brown, 20 to 25 minutes. Sprinkle with the parsley and serve hot, with the lemon wedges.

Roasted Salmon with Pomegranate Butter Sauce

If you've never roasted salmon, get ready for a treat, as the oven heat seals in the flavor better than moist-heat methods like poaching or steaming. It isn't fancy; that is, until it comes into contact with this special sauce, a red variation of the classic *beurre blanc*. One important tip: Incorporate the butter over very low heat so it softens into a creamy emulsion with the acidic base. If the heat is too high, the butter will simply melt. While the sauce is made with bottled pomegranate juice, garnish each serving with a few pomegranate seeds, if you wish.

One 2-pound center-cut salmon fillet, with skin

½ teaspoon salt

¼ teaspoon freshly ground black pepper

POMEGRANATE BUTTER SAUCE

½ cup bottled pomegranate juice

½ cup hearty red wine, such as Syrah-Cabernet blend

2 tablespoons minced shallots

½ teaspoon chopped fresh rosemary or ¼ teaspoon crumbled dried rosemary

8 tablespoons (1 stick) unsalted butter, chilled, cut into 8 equal portions

Salt and freshly ground black pepper

1. Preheat the oven to 400°F. Lightly oil a large rimmed baking sheet.

2. Run your fingers over the cut side of the salmon, feeling for any pin bones. If necessary, pull out the bones with sterilized tweezers. Place the salmon on the baking sheet, flesh side up. Season with the salt and pepper. Cut the salmon vertically into 6 equal portions, but do not separate the pieces. (This makes the salmon easier to serve after cooking.)

3. Roast until the salmon shows just a hint of bright pink when prodded in the center of the fillet at one of the cuts with the tip of a knife, 12 to 15 minutes.

4. Meanwhile, make the butter sauce. Bring the pomegranate juice, wine, shallots, and rosemary to a boil in a nonreactive medium saucepan over high heat. Cook until the liquid is reduced to 2 tablespoons, about 6 minutes. Reduce the heat to very low.

5. Remove the pan from the heat and whisk in 1 tablespoon of the butter. Whisk until the butter softens into a creamy texture, occasionally returning the pan to the heat to keep it warm, but not hot. Repeat with the remaining butter, 1 tablespoon at a time. Season with salt and pepper to taste. If you wish, strain the sauce through a coarse-mesh wire strainer into a serving bowl, but I usually skip this refinement, as the sauce will taste great one way or the other. Do not bother to try to keep the sauce piping hot; it will be heated by the warmth of the salmon.

6. Serve the salmon on individual dinner plates, and spoon the sauce on top. Serve immediately.

Roasted Loin of Pork with Brussels Sprouts

Makes 6 to 8 servings

The scent of this roasting pork reminds me of Sunday suppers past, although no one in my family ever thought of roasting the Brussels sprouts in the pan juices, a technique that will make the most delicious sprouts you've ever had. And that's a promise. Although boneless pork roasts are easy to find, there is a huge improvement in flavor when the meat is cooked on the bone, so don't compromise.

3 tablespoons extra-virgin olive oil, divided, plus more for the pan

One 4-pound center-cut pork loin with bones

1 teaspoon crumbled dried rosemary

1 teaspoon rubbed dried sage

1 teaspoon dried thyme

½ teaspoon ground fennel seed (grind in an electric grinder or mortar and pestle)

1 teaspoon kosher salt, plus more to taste

½ teaspoon freshly ground black pepper, plus more to taste

Three 10-ounce containers Brussels sprouts, each sprout trimmed and cut in half vertically

¾ cup canned low-sodium chicken broth

2 tablespoons dry sherry

1 tablespoon unsalted butter, chilled

1. Preheat the oven to 350°F. Lightly oil a large roasting pan.

2. Massage the pork loin all over with 1 tablespoon of the oil. Mix together the rosemary, sage, thyme, fennel seed, 1 teaspoon salt, and ½ teaspoon pepper and sprinkle all over the pork. Place the roast, bones down, in the pan. Roast until an instant-read meat thermometer inserted in the center of the roast reads 120°F, about 1 hour.

3. Toss the Brussels sprouts with the remaining 2 tablespoons oil in a large bowl. Season lightly with salt and pepper. Remove the pan from the oven, scatter the Brussels sprouts in the pan around the roast, and stir well to coat them with the pan juices. Return to the oven. Continue roasting until the pork reads 145°F when tested again with the meat thermometer, about 25 minutes. Transfer the roast to a serving platter and tent with aluminum foil.

4. Stir the Brussels sprouts in the pan, and return to the oven. Continue roasting until the sprouts are tender, about 15 minutes longer. Transfer to the platter with the roast. Carve the roast and shingle the slices over the sprouts.

5. Place the roasting pan on the stove over two burners on medium heat and cook until the pan juices sizzle. Add the broth and sherry and bring to a boil, stirring up the browned bits in the bottom and sides of the pan with a wooden spatula. Remove from the heat and stir in the butter to melt and lightly thicken the sauce. Season with salt and pepper to taste. Pour over the pork and serve immediately.

Brussels Sprouts

If you think that Brussels sprouts look like little cabbages on a stalk, you would be right, as both are members of the Brassica genus, otherwise known as cruciferous for their four-petal, cross-shaped flowers. These vegetables were originally an important crop in what is now Belgium, hence their name.

Like many other fruits and vegetables, different varieties have been cultivated to keep Brussels sprouts available year-round. However, they are traditionally harvested in the fall, and they are especially valuable to farmers because they can be grown in temperatures as low as 45°F. Once harvested, the sprouts keep very well at near-freezing temperatures.

Choose Brussels sprouts that are firm and green, and pass over ones with tiny brown holes, which could mean that they are housing bugs. Rinse them well and remove any wilted leaves. Give the bases a trim, and you're all set for cooking.

Brussels sprouts are often cooked whole or halved. However, for a quick side dish, thinly slice the sprouts crosswise (a food processor fitted with the slicing blade makes very short work of this), and sauté them in a little butter or oil until barely tender.

Oktoberfest Sausages and Red Cabbage

Makes 6 servings

Here's a dish that is a classic of German cooking, and worthy of an Oktoberfest celebration. In my maternal grandmother's kitchen, it didn't have to be October for her to make sausages in red cabbage. She came from Liechtenstein, and she cooked solid German fare for her seven children. I learned early in my cooking life not to try and rush the cabbage, as it needs plenty of time to soften into the melting mass of sweet and sour ingredients that makes it so unique, and to become the perfect bed on which to cook your favorite sausages. Of course, chill some beer to drink with this meal!

RED CABBAGE AND APPLES

3 tablespoons vegetable oil, divided

6 slices thick-sliced bacon, coarsely chopped

1 large onion, thinly sliced

2 Golden Delicious apples, peeled, cored, and cut into ¼-inch-thick wedges

One 2½-pound head red cabbage, cut into wedges, core removed, and thinly sliced

One 12-ounce bottle hard cider (see Note)

⅓ cup cider vinegar

½ cup packed light brown sugar

½ teaspoon dried thyme

1 bay leaf

Salt and freshly ground black pepper

12 assorted sausages, such as bratwurst, weisswurst, hot links, and knockwurst, pricked with a fork

1. To make the red cabbage and apples, heat 1 tablespoon of the oil in a very large Dutch oven or flame-proof casserole over medium heat. Add the bacon and cook, stirring occasionally, until crisp and browned, about 8 minutes. Using a slotted spoon, transfer to paper towels to drain, leaving the fat in the pan.

2. Add the onion and cook, stirring often, until golden, about 10 minutes. Transfer to a bowl. Add the remaining 2 tablespoons of oil to the Dutch oven and heat until hot but not smoking. Add the apples and cook, stirring often, until lightly browned, about 3 minutes. Add the cabbage, cider, vinegar, brown sugar, thyme, and bay leaf and stir well to coat the cabbage with the liquid. (The vinegar helps the cabbage hold

its color.) Bring to a boil over high heat. Reduce the heat to medium-low and cover. Simmer, stirring occasionally, until the cabbage is tender, about 1½ hours. Season with salt and pepper to taste.

3. Bury the sausages in the cabbage and cover. Cook until they are heated through, about 12 minutes. Using a slotted spoon, transfer the cabbage and sausages to a large serving bowl, removing the bay leaf, and tent with aluminum foil. Bring the cooking liquid in the pot to a boil over high heat and cook, stirring often, until reduced to about ½ cup, about 5 minutes. Pour over the cabbage and sausages and serve hot.

Note

Hard cider is a fermented alcoholic cider, available bottled at liquor stores. I always have it in my refrigerator for drinking and cooking, especially in the fall. For a substitute, use equal amounts of apple juice and white wine (either dry or fruity), or apple juice alone.

An Oktoberfest Supper

Celery Root and Red Pepper Slaw (page 35)

Oktoberfest Sausages and Red Cabbage (page 84)

Oven-roasted potatoes (recipe not included)

Apple Kuchen (page 153)

Chilled beer

PASTA AND RISOTTO

Baked Pasta with Gruyère and Mushrooms

Fettuccine with Roasted Butternut Squash and Chard

Ziti with Chicken, Broccoli, and Rosemary

Polenta "Pizza" with Wild Mushrooms and Fontina

Broccoli Rabe and Sausage Risotto

Chicken Cacciatore Ragù on Creamy Polenta

Baked Pasta with Gruyère and Mushrooms

Think of this as French macaroni and cheese. Or, as the most outrageous macaroni and cheese you'll ever eat. It is worth the extra time at the gym.

5 tablespoons (½ stick plus 1 tablespoon) unsalted butter, divided, plus more for the dish

2 tablespoons vegetable oil

1 pound cremini (baby bella) mushrooms, quartered

Salt and freshly ground black pepper

1 pound tubular pasta, such as penne, ziti, or cavatappi

¼ cup all-purpose flour

3 cups whole milk, heated

3 cups (12 ounces) shredded Gruyère cheese

½ cup panko (Japanese bread crumbs) or coarse bread crumbs, made from day-old bread in a food processor

1. Position a rack in the center of the oven and preheat the oven to 350°F. Lightly butter a 3-quart shallow baking dish.

2. Heat the oil in a very large skillet over medium-high heat. Add the mushrooms and cook, stirring occasionally, until the mushrooms are lightly browned, about 10 minutes. Season with salt and pepper. Set aside.

3. Meanwhile, bring a large pot of lightly salted water to a boil over high heat. Add the pasta and cook according to the package instructions until it is not quite al dente (it will cook more in the oven). Drain.

4. Return the pasta pot to medium heat. Add 4 tablespoons of the butter and melt. Whisk in the flour and reduce the heat to low. Let the roux bubble without browning for 1 minute. Whisk in the hot milk and bring to a boil over high heat. Stir in the Gruyère. Remove from the heat. Stir in the pasta and mushrooms, and season with salt and pepper. Spread in the baking dish. Sprinkle with the bread crumbs. Cut the remaining 1 tablespoon butter into small cubes and dot over the bread crumbs. Bake until the topping is brown and the sauce is bubbling, about 25 minutes. Serve hot.

Fettuccine with Roasted Butternut Squash and Chard

Makes 6 servings

This filling pasta is literally autumn on a plate, with roasted squash, earthy chard, and salty pancetta playing off one another. Serve it as a main course, or in smaller portions to start off a more elegant repast.

2¼ pounds butternut squash, peeled, seeded, and cut into 1-inch cubes

2 tablespoons extra-virgin olive oil, divided

½ teaspoon salt, plus more to taste

¼ teaspoon freshly ground black pepper, plus more to taste

1 bunch Swiss chard, preferably red or rainbow

4 ounces thick-cut pancetta, coarsely chopped

1 red onion, chopped

2 garlic cloves, finely chopped

2 cups canned low-sodium chicken broth

1 pound fettuccine

½ cup (2 ounces) freshly grated Parmesan cheese, plus more for serving

1. Position a rack in the center of the oven and preheat the oven to 400°F. Lightly oil a rimmed baking sheet.

2. Toss the squash with 1 tablespoon of the oil, ½ teaspoon salt, and ¼ teaspoon pepper. Spread on the baking sheet. Roast, stirring occasionally, until the squash is browned and tender, about 1 hour.

3. Meanwhile, prepare the chard. Strip the leafy tops from the stems and reserve separately. Wash the stems well in a sink of cold water. Transfer to a chopping board, shaking off excess water, but do not dry. Cut the stems into ½-inch lengths. Repeat with the tops, cutting them into ½-inch-wide strips.

4. Heat the remaining 1 tablespoon oil in a large saucepan over medium-low heat. Add the pancetta and cook, stirring often, until it is crisp and golden brown, about 8 minutes. Using a slotted spoon, transfer the pancetta to a bowl, leaving the fat in the skillet. Add the onion and cook, stirring occasionally, until lightly browned, about 5 minutes. Stir in the garlic and cook until fragrant, about 1 minute. Add the chard stems and increase the heat to medium-high. Cook until beginning to soften, about 2 minutes. Stir in the chard tops, return the heat to medium-low, and cover. Cook, stirring occasionally, until the chard is tender, about 15 minutes. Stir in the broth and bring to a boil. Keep warm.

5. Bring a large pot of lightly salted water to a boil over high heat. Add the fettuccine and cook according to the package instructions until the pasta is al dente. Drain. Return the pasta to its warm cooking pot.

6. Add the chard mixture, roasted squash, and the ½ cup of Parmesan cheese. Mix well and season with salt and pepper. Serve hot, with a bowl of Parmesan cheese passed on the side.

Ziti with Chicken, Broccoli, and Rosemary

Makes 6 servings

Chicken isn't always the best match with pasta. But this dish, created out of desperation to make a meal that some very picky young friends of mine might like, scores. Leave out the wine, if you wish.

4 cups broccoli florets

2 tablespoons olive oil, plus more as needed

½ cup all-purpose flour

½ teaspoon salt, plus more to taste

½ teaspoon freshly ground black pepper, plus more to taste

12 ounces boneless and skinless chicken breasts, cut into strips
about 1 inch wide and 2 inches long

2 tablespoons unsalted butter

1 garlic clove, minced

1 cup canned low-sodium chicken broth

1 cup heavy cream

⅓ cup dry white wine

2 teaspoons chopped fresh rosemary

1 pound ziti or other tubular pasta

1 cup shredded sharp Cheddar cheese

Freshly grated Parmesan cheese, for serving

1. Bring a large pot of lightly salted water to a boil over high heat. Add the broccoli to the water and cook until crisp-tender, about 4 minutes. Lift out the broccoli with a wire sieve or skimmer, and transfer to a bowl. Set aside.

2. Meanwhile, start the pasta sauce. Heat the oil in a large skillet over medium heat. Mix the flour with $\frac{1}{2}$ teaspoon each of salt and pepper in a shallow dish. Toss half of the chicken strips in the flour, shake off the excess, and add the chicken to the skillet. Cook, occasionally turning the chicken, until lightly browned, about 3 minutes. Transfer to a plate. Repeat with the remaining chicken, adding more oil to the skillet as needed. Reserve 1 tablespoon of the seasoned flour and discard the rest.

3. Add the butter to the skillet and melt over medium heat. Add the garlic and cook until fragrant, about 1 minute. Whisk in the reserved flour. Reduce the heat to medium-low and let bubble without browning for 30 seconds. Whisk in the broth, cream, wine, and rosemary and bring to a boil over high heat, scraping up any browned bits in the pan with a wooden spoon. Return the chicken to the skillet, and return the heat to medium-low. Simmer until the chicken is cooked through, about 10 minutes.

4. While the sauce is simmering, bring the same water in which the broccoli was cooked back to a boil, add the pasta, and cook according to the instructions on the package until al dente. During the last minute or so, return the broccoli to the pot to heat through. Drain well.

5. Return the pasta and broccoli to the pot, add the chicken and sauce and the Cheddar cheese, and mix well. Season with salt and pepper. Serve hot, with a bowl of the Parmesan cheese passed on the side.

Polenta "Pizza" with Wild Mushrooms and Fontina

Makes 6 servings

Cooled polenta is firm enough to become a base for toppings like the mushrooms and Fontina here. Try this concept another time with roasted butternut squash, caramelized onions, and Gorgonzola.

POLENTA

Extra-virgin olive oil, for the baking dish

2 teaspoons salt

1⅓ cups instant polenta

2 tablespoons extra-virgin olive oil

½ pound cremini (baby bella) mushrooms, sliced

¼ pound shiitake mushrooms, stemmed, caps sliced

¼ pound oyster mushrooms, trimmed and sliced

¼ cup minced shallots

2 garlic cloves, minced

2 ripe plum tomatoes, seeded and cut into ¼-inch dice

1 teaspoon chopped fresh rosemary

1 teaspoon chopped fresh thyme

Salt and freshly ground black pepper

1½ cups (6 ounces) shredded Fontina cheese, preferably Fontina d'Aosta

1. Position an oven rack in the upper third of the oven and preheat to 400°F. Lightly oil a 13 x 9-inch baking dish.

2. To prepare the polenta, bring 4 cups water and the salt to a boil in a medium saucepan over high heat. Whisk in the polenta and reduce the heat to medium-low. Cook, whisking often, until it is very thick, about 3 minutes. Spread evenly in the dish. Place the dish on a wire cake rack and let stand until tepid and firmed, about 20 minutes.

3. Heat the 2 tablespoons oil in a large skillet over medium-high heat. Add the cremini, shiitake, and oyster mushrooms and cook, stirring often, until the mushroom juices extrude and evaporate, about 10 minutes. Stir in the shallots and garlic and cook until they are fragrant, about 1 minute. Stir in the tomatoes, rosemary, and thyme. Season with salt and pepper to taste.

4. Scatter the mushroom mixture over the polenta. Sprinkle with the Fontina. Bake until the cheese is melted, about 15 minutes. Cut into rectangles and serve hot.

Broccoli Rabe and Sausage Risotto

Makes 4 to 6 servings

Broccoli rabe has a frankly bitter flavor that is mellowed by the addition of Italian sausage. When the combination is stirred into risotto, the bitterness is tempered even further. Serve it hot from the pot. The risotto will firm up if allowed to stand.

1 tablespoon extra-virgin olive oil

1 pound sweet or hot Italian sausage, casings removed

2 garlic cloves, minced

1 bunch broccoli rabe, about 1¼ pounds

¼ teaspoon crushed hot red pepper

6 cups canned low-sodium chicken broth, as needed

2 tablespoons unsalted butter

1 medium onion, chopped

2 cups rice for risotto, such as Arborio, Vialone Nano, or Carnaroli

1 cup dry white wine

½ cup (2 ounces) freshly grated Parmesan cheese, plus more for serving

Salt and freshly ground black pepper

1 cup (4 ounces) crumbled ricotta salata cheese

1. Heat the oil in a large, wide skillet over medium-high heat. Add the sausage and cook, stirring and breaking up the sausage with a spoon, until it is lightly browned, about 10 minutes. Add the garlic and cook until it is fragrant, about 1 minute.

2. While the sausage is cooking, rinse the broccoli rabe well. Transfer to a cutting board (do not dry) and coarsely chop the broccoli rabe. When the garlic is fragrant, in batches, letting the first batch wilt before adding another, stir the broccoli rabe into the skillet and add the hot pepper. Cover and reduce the heat to medium-low. Cook until the broccoli rabe is very tender, about 20 minutes.

3. Meanwhile, bring the broth and 2 cups water to a boil in a medium saucepan over high heat. Reduce the heat to very low to keep the broth mixture hot.

4. Melt the butter in a heavy-bottomed, large saucepan over medium heat. Add the onion and cook, stirring often, until softened, about 4 minutes. Add the rice and cook, stirring often, until it turns from translucent to opaque and feels somewhat heavier in the spoon (do not brown), about 2 minutes. Add the wine and cook until almost evaporated, about 2 minutes.

5. About 1 cup at a time, stir the hot broth into the rice. Reduce the heat to medium-low so the rice cooks at a steady simmer. Cook, stirring almost constantly, until the rice absorbs almost all of the stock, about 3 minutes. Stir in another cup of stock, and stir until it is almost absorbed. Repeat, keeping the risotto at a steady simmer and adding more stock as it is absorbed, until you use all of the stock and the rice is barely tender, about 20 minutes total. If you run out of stock and the rice isn't quite tender, use hot water. When the risotto is almost done, stir in the broccoli rabe and sausage mixture, and then the ½ cup of Parmesan cheese. Season with salt and pepper to taste. Just before serving, stir in a final addition of broth; the risotto will have a loose, flowing consistency.

6. Spoon the risotto into individual bowls, and top each serving with the ricotta salata. Serve hot, with a bowl of additional Parmesan cheese passed at the table.

Chicken Cacciatore Ragù on Creamy Polenta

Makes 4 to 6 servings

Here are all the flavors of the traditional chicken cacciatore, but made more quickly with boneless and skinless chicken thighs. Spooned over a big bowl of creamy polenta, this is comfort food made for an autumn evening.

RAGÙ

3 tablespoons extra-virgin olive oil, divided

2 pounds boneless and skinless chicken thighs, cut into 1-inch pieces

1 teaspoon salt, plus more to taste

½ teaspoon freshly ground black pepper, plus more to taste

10 ounces cremini (baby bella) mushrooms, quartered

1 medium onion, finely chopped

2 garlic cloves, minced

½ cup hearty red wine

One 28-ounce can diced tomatoes in juice

One 8-ounce can tomato sauce

2 teaspoons dried porcini powder (optional)

1 teaspoon dried rosemary

1 teaspoon dried basil

CREAMY POLENTA

1 cup whole milk

2 teaspoons salt

1⅓ cups instant polenta

½ cup freshly grated Parmesan cheese, plus more for serving

1. To make the ragù, heat 2 tablespoons of the oil in a large saucepan. Season the chicken with 1 teaspoon salt and ½ teaspoon pepper. In batches without crowding, add the chicken and cook, turning occasionally, until browned, about 5 minutes. Using a slotted spoon, leaving the fat in the saucepan, transfer the chicken to a plate.

2. Add the remaining 1 tablespoon of oil to the saucepan and heat. Add the mushrooms and cook, stirring occasionally with a wooden spatula as the mushrooms give off their juices to loosen the browned bits in the saucepan, until the mushrooms begin to brown, about 3 minutes. Add the onion and cook, stirring occasionally, until softened, about 3 minutes. Stir in the garlic and cook until fragrant, about 1 minute.

3. Add the wine and cook, stirring up the browned bits in the bottom of the pan. Stir in the tomatoes and their juice, the tomato sauce, porcini powder, if using, and the rosemary and basil. Bring to a simmer. Return the chicken, with its juices, to the pan. Reduce the heat to medium-low and simmer, stirring occasionally, until the chicken is cooked through, about 45 minutes. Season with salt and pepper.

4. About 5 minutes before the ragù is done, make the polenta. Bring 3 cups water, the milk, and the salt to a boil in a heavy-bottomed medium saucepan over high heat. Whisk in the polenta and reduce the heat to medium-low. Cook, whisking often, until the polenta is thick, about 2 minutes. Remove from the heat and stir in the ½ cup of Parmesan cheese.

5. Spoon the hot polenta into individual serving bowls and top with the ragù. Serve hot, with a bowl of Parmesan passed on the side.

SIDE DISHES

Cornbread Stuffing with Dried Fruits and Hazelnuts

Italian-Style Stuffing with Sausage, Fennel, and Mushrooms

Baked Cardoons in Fontina Sauce

Cranberry and Sage Cornbread

Green Beans with Caramelized Shallot Butter

Mashed Potatoes with Mascarpone and Roasted Garlic

Roasted Yams with Orange-Chipotle Glaze

Gratin of Parsnips and Celery Root

Cranberry Rum-Raisin Sauce

Cornbread Stuffing with Dried Fruits and Hazelnuts

Makes 12 to 16 servings

There is one thing that I have learned about stuffing (call it dressing, if you wish) after making hundreds of Thanksgiving dinners in my annual holiday cooking classes: Keep it basic. Every time I serve something too upscale, I get in trouble. For a traditional stuffing that hits all the right notes, try this cornbread version. The eggs help the stuffing hold together, making for easier serving, but they can be deleted, if you prefer.

2 batches Cranberry and Sage Cornbread (page 115)

Two 5-ounce packages mixed dried fruit, such as apricots, pears, peaches, and pitted dried plums

8 tablespoons (½ stick) unsalted butter

1 large onion, chopped

5 celery ribs, cut into ½-inch dice

3 tablespoons chopped fresh parsley

2 teaspoons crumbled dried rosemary

1 teaspoon dried thyme

1 teaspoon celery seed

1½ cups Turkey Stock (page 44) or canned low-sodium chicken broth, as needed

Salt and freshly ground black pepper

2 large eggs, beaten (optional)

1 cup toasted and coarsely chopped hazelnuts

1. The day before making the stuffing, bake and cool the cornbreads. Crumble them onto a large baking sheet. Let stand overnight, uncovered, to dry and stale.

2. Combine the dried fruit and enough warm water to cover in a medium bowl. Let stand until softened, about 1 hour. Drain well. Cut the fruit into bite-size pieces.

3. Melt the butter in a large skillet over medium-high heat. Add the onion and celery and cook, stirring often, until tender, about 10 minutes. Transfer to a large bowl. Add the cornbread, drained fruit, parsley, rosemary, thyme, and celery seed. Stir in enough of the stock to thoroughly moisten the stuffing, about 1½ cups. Season with salt and pepper to taste. Beat the eggs, if using, in a small bowl and stir into the stuffing. Stir in the hazelnuts. Use immediately as a turkey stuffing.

Italian-Style Stuffing with Sausage, Fennel, and Mushrooms

Makes about 12 cups, 12 to 16 servings

I can't resist adding another stuffing, knowing that they are so popular at Thanksgiving. This Italian-inspired offering has the fall flavors of sausage, fennel, and mushrooms, brightened with sweet red bell pepper and Parmesan. For the best texture, use bread with a firm, not open, crumb. Most basic Italian or French loaves work fine, but ciabatta has too many holes.

3 tablespoons olive oil, divided

1 pound sweet Italian sausage, casings removed

2 small heads fennel, cut into ½-inch dice (3 cups)

1 large onion, chopped

1 large red bell pepper, seeded, cored, and cut into ½-inch dice

10 ounces cremini (baby bella) mushrooms, sliced

4 garlic cloves, chopped

1 pound day-old, crusty Italian or French bread with a firm crumb, cut into 1-inch cubes (8 cups)

1 cup freshly grated Parmesan cheese

2 tablespoons chopped fresh rosemary

1½ cups Turkey Stock (page 44), as needed

Salt and freshly ground black pepper

1. Heat 1 tablespoon of the oil in a large skillet over medium-high heat. Add the sausage and cook, breaking up the sausage with the side of a spoon, until the sausage is cooked through, about 10 minutes. Using a slotted spoon, transfer the sausage to a large bowl, leaving the fat in the pan.

2. Add the fennel and onion to the skillet and reduce the heat to medium. Cover and cook, stirring occasionally, until the fennel is tender, about 10 minutes. Transfer to the bowl with the sausage.

3. Add the remaining 2 tablespoons of oil to the skillet and heat. Add the bell pepper and cook until it begins to soften, about 3 minutes. Add the mushrooms and cook, stirring occasionally, until the mushroom juices evaporate and the mushrooms begin to brown, about 12 minutes. Stir in the garlic and cook until it is fragrant, about 1 minute. Transfer to the bowl with the sausage and vegetables.

4. Add the bread cubes, Parmesan, and rosemary. Stir in enough stock to moisten the cornbread, about 1½ cups. Season with the salt and pepper to taste. Use immediately as a turkey stuffing.

Baked Cardoons in Fontina Sauce

Makes 4 to 6 servings

Every November cardoons appear with clockwork precision at my supermarket. Whenever I pick up a bunch, another shopper always stops me to ask what the heck the scary-looking stalks are and how to cook them. This is my favorite recipe to introduce the uninitiated to this mellow-flavored vegetable. While I have considered experimenting with them, I go back to this classic rendition of blanched cardoons baked in a creamy cheese sauce. Serve it as a rich side dish to a simple roast.

2 tablespoons unsalted butter, divided, plus more for the baking dish

2 tablespoons white wine vinegar or white distilled vinegar

3 or 4 large cardoon stalks (about 1 ½ pounds)

1 tablespoon all-purpose flour

1 cup whole milk, heated

½ cup (2 ounces) shredded Fontina cheese, preferably Fontina d'Aosta

Salt and freshly ground black pepper

2 tablespoons freshly grated Parmesan cheese

1. Position a rack in the top third of the oven and preheat the oven to 350°F. Lightly butter a shallow 1-quart baking dish.

2. Bring a medium saucepan of lightly salted water to a boil and add the vinegar. Meanwhile, clean the cardoons. Run a vegetable peeler lengthwise down each cardoon to peel them, being sure to use enough pressure to completely remove

the thick stringy ridges and reveal the pale flesh under the skin. Cut the cardoons into 3- to 4-inch lengths. Add to the acidulated water and cook until barely tender, about 5 minutes. Drain.

3. Melt 1 tablespoon of the butter in a medium saucepan over medium heat. Whisk in the flour and reduce the heat to low. Let bubble without browning for 1 minute. Whisk in the milk, return the heat to medium, and bring to a simmer. Simmer, whisking often, and adjusting the heat as needed to keep the sauce from scorching, until smooth and thickened, about 2 minutes. Remove from the heat, add the Fontina, and stir until melted. Season with salt and pepper.

4. Spread the cardoons in the baking dish and spread the sauce over the top. Sprinkle with the Parmesan. Cut the remaining 1 tablespoon of butter into small pieces and dot over the sauce. Bake until the top is golden brown, about 25 minutes. Serve hot.

Cardoons

I live in an area rich with Italian-American heritage. For a few weeks every November and December, an odd-looking vegetable—looking like pale celery on steroids—appears in the produce section of my supermarket. The staff is kept busy restocking the bin, for the supply disappears quickly as knowledgeable cooks snap it up. This tasty vegetable is the cardoon.

The cardoon is a member of the thistle family, and its flesh tastes similar to artichoke hearts. Some varieties have small spikes sticking out of the thick skin, and although most commercial crops are spike-free, take care when peeling; rubber gloves may be in order. Cardoons have a very long growing season that extends into fall, making them an autumn crop. However, they are sensitive to frost, so they show up in the market before the weather turns really cold.

Cardoons take a little preparation before eating. Like artichokes, they are cooked in acidulated (vinegar or lemon juice) water to discourage discoloration. Precooking in water reduces their bitterness. They are very popular dipped in batter and deep-fried, but I am partial to baking them in a cheese sauce (page 112). When you see them, if you aren't Italian, act like you are and buy some to make an unusual addition to your fall bill of fare.

Cranberry and Sage Cornbread

Makes 6 to 8 servings

Freshly baked cornbread is so easy to prepare that there seems to be no real reason for the packaged stuff to exist. And, especially if you are making a cornbread stuffing for a holiday turkey, the boxed mix is too sweet. This sweet-and-savory quick bread works on its own to fill out a menu, or as the basis of a great dressing to fill your bird. If you like your cornbread on the sweet side, use the sugar, but use unsweetened cornbread for a stuffing.

1 ¼ cups yellow cornmeal, preferably stone-ground

¾ cups all-purpose flour

3 tablespoons sugar (optional)

2 teaspoons baking powder

½ teaspoon salt

3 tablespoons unsalted butter

1 cup whole milk

1 large egg, beaten

½ cup dried cranberries

1 tablespoon finely chopped fresh sage

1. Position a rack in the center of the oven and preheat the oven to 400°F.

2. Whisk together the cornmeal, flour, sugar, if using, baking powder, and salt in a medium bowl and make a well in the center.

3. Place the butter in an 8-inch square baking dish and place in the oven to melt the butter and heat the dish, about 3 minutes.

4. Whisk together the milk and egg in a small bowl. Whisk the melted butter from the baking dish into the milk mixture. Pour into the well in the dry ingredients and stir just until blended; a few lumps may remain. Do not overmix. Fold in the cranberries and sage. Spread evenly in the hot baking dish and return to the oven.

5. Bake until golden brown and the top of the bread springs back when pressed in the center, about 20 minutes. Let cool for 5 minutes, then cut into squares to serve hot or warm.

Variation

Cranberry and Sage Cornbread for Stuffing: Double the ingredients, leave out the sugar, and bake in a 15 x 10-inch baking dish for about 25 minutes.

Cranberries

Originally called craneberry because its long blossom resembled the head and bill of a crane, this tart red berry adds zip to many autumn dishes. However, cranberries can be a bit too tangy, so don't use them indiscriminately without adding sugar or another sweetener, too. While some people stir raw cranberries into batter and doughs for baked goods, I find their sourness very distracting, and I prefer to use sweetened dried cranberries for this purpose.

Young cranberries are white, and they only turn red when fully ripe. If you have ever wondered where clear white cranberry juice comes from, it is processed from immature berries.

Cranberries are great keepers. Refrigerated in their bags, they will remain fresh for a month or so after purchase, and they can be frozen for up to a year. If you do like cranberries in your baked goods, and use frozen berries, the berries will chill the batter, so allow an extra few minutes of baking time. Before using, rinse the fresh cranberries in a colander and sort through them, discarding any shriveled or soft berries. If using frozen berries, rinse them very briefly, and pat them dry with paper towels before proceeding, but do not let them thaw.

Green Beans with Caramelized Shallot Butter

Makes 8 servings

Green beans are not in season everywhere in the fall, but they get a deeper, more satisfying flavor from a good amount of shallots, which are part of the traditional autumn harvest. This light, fresh-tasting dish is almost always on my holiday table to act as relief to the other heavy-hitters being served. A bit of the cooking water combines with the butter to make a lovely sauce.

CARAMELIZED SHALLOT BUTTER

5 tablespoons unsalted butter (4 tablespoons softened)

4 shallots, coarsely chopped (1 cup)

1 ½ pounds green beans, trimmed and cut into 2-inch lengths

Salt and freshly ground black pepper

1. To make the caramelized shallot butter, heat 1 tablespoon of the butter in a medium skillet over medium-low heat. Add the shallots and cook, stirring occasionally, until the shallots are lightly browned and tender, adjusting the temperature as needed to avoid scorching, about 20 minutes. Transfer to a small bowl and cool. Add the softened butter and stir to combine. (The shallot butter can be prepared up to 3 days ahead, covered, and refrigerated. Bring to room temperature before using.)

2. Bring a large pot of lightly salted water to a boil over high heat. Add the green beans and cook until just tender, about 5 minutes. Reserve ⅓ cup of the cooking water. Drain the green beans. Return them to the cooking pot and add the shallot butter and the reserved cooking water. Mix well, until the butter melts. Season with salt and pepper to taste. Transfer to a warmed serving bowl and serve hot.

Mashed Potatoes with Mascarpone and Roasted Garlic

Makes 8 to 10 servings

Mascarpone is a thick, creamy cheese that can transform mundane mashed potatoes into something luxurious. Be sure to remove the cheese from the refrigerator at least an hour ahead of time so it can lose its chill before mashing, or else you'll end up with lukewarm potatoes.

3 pounds baking potatoes, such as russet or Burbank, peeled and cut into 2-inch chunks

1 large head roasted garlic (see page 16)

½ pound mascarpone cheese, at room temperature

Salt and freshly ground black pepper

1. Put the potato chunks in a large pot and add enough lightly salted, cold water to cover by 1 inch. Cover and bring to a boil over high heat. Reduce the heat to medium and simmer briskly until the potatoes are tender, about 25 minutes. Drain well. Return the potatoes to the pot and stir over medium-low heat for about 2 minutes to remove excess moisture. Remove from the heat.

2. Squeeze the roasted garlic from the hulls into the potatoes. Add the mascarpone. Using an electric hand mixer on high speed, beat until smooth. Season with salt and pepper to taste. Transfer to a warmed serving bowl and serve hot.

Roasted Yams with Orange-Chipotle Glaze

Makes 8 servings

Yams (call them sweet potatoes if you wish, but those have ivory-colored white flesh and aren't as sugary as yams) are a must for a Thanksgiving side dish. But, these are so easy to prepare that you may find yourself making them to serve alongside other main courses, such as baked ham.

3 pounds slender orange-fleshed yams, such as jewel, garnet, or Louisiana, peeled

3 tablespoons extra-virgin olive oil

2 tablespoons unsalted butter, softened

2 tablespoons bitter orange marmalade

Grated zest of 1 large orange

¼ teaspoon pure ground chipotle chile (see Note)

Salt

1. Position a rack in the top third of the oven and preheat the oven to 400°F. Line an 18 x 13-inch rimmed baking sheet (such as a "half-sheet") with aluminum foil.

2. Cut each yam in half lengthwise, then crosswise into ¾-inch-thick half-rounds. Toss the yams on the baking sheet with the oil and spread into a single layer.

3. Bake, turning the yams occasionally with a metal spatula, until the yams are tender and lightly browned, about 30 minutes. (The yams can be prepared up to 8 hours ahead, cooled, and stored on the baking sheet at room temperature. Reheat for 5 minutes in a preheated 400°F oven before proceeding.)

4. Meanwhile, mash the butter, marmalade, orange zest, and ground chipotle chile in a small bowl and set aside at room temperature. (The orange butter can be prepared up to 3 hours ahead and stored at room temperature.)

5. Remove the yams from the oven. Dollop heaping teaspoons of the orange butter over the yams and stir gently to coat. Return the yams to the oven and bake until the orange butter reduces to a glaze, about 5 minutes. Season lightly with salt to taste. Transfer to a warmed serving bowl and serve hot.

Note

For this recipe, use ground dried chipotle, available at Latino markets and most supermarkets, not the canned ones in adobo sauce. (Both Spice Islands and McCormick's stock ground chipotle, so look in their displays at your market.) If you wish, substitute 1/2 teaspoon pure ground ancho chile (which is milder and sweeter) or 1 teaspoon chili powder (a mild ground chile base mixed with cumin and oregano) for the chipotle.

Yams

Orange-fleshed yams are a familiar sight on autumn tables, as they are the side dish of choice to go with a holiday roast turkey or ham. Even though everyone I know uses the terms interchangeably, sweet potatoes are not yams.

The truth is, a true sweet potato has ivory flesh with a purplish skin. It is also known as *boniato* or *batata*. A yam is orange-fleshed with pale brown skin. A few varieties are available, with the choice widening around Thanksgiving. Louisiana yams are the most common, but look for the smaller, narrower jewel or garnet varieties, which have a slightly firmer interior. A true yam has a scaly brown skin and is called *ñame* by Spanish-speaking cooks. Neither the sweet potato nor the ñame is particularly sweet. My supermarket, being in a multiethnic neighborhood, carries orange yams, sweet potatoes, and ñames. More than once, when I sent someone else shopping for my groceries and asked for sweet potatoes, I got orange yams, and when I asked for yams, I got ñames. Now I draw a picture on the shopping list and hope for the best.

Yams are not related to potatoes, and they do not keep especially well. They should be stored not at room temperature, but in the refrigerator, for up to a week before using.

Gratin of Parsnips and Celery Root

Makes 6 to 8 servings

Root vegetables such as parsnips and celery root (celeriac) have a sweet undertone that seems to welcome other rich ingredients. Here, the vegetables are simply baked with lots of cream into a golden brown marriage made in heaven. Neither of the vegetables is overly familiar to my friends, and I love serving this and making new friends for them.

2 large parsnips, about 1 pound

1 large celery root, about 1 pound

1 teaspoon salt

½ teaspoon freshly ground black pepper

2 ½ cups heavy cream

1. Position a rack in the top third of the oven and preheat to 400°F. Lightly butter an 11 ½ x 8-inch baking dish.

2. Peel the parsnips and cut them into 1-inch chunks. Peel the celery root and cut it into 1-inch chunks, discarding any soft or woody spots. Toss the vegetables in a bowl with the salt and pepper. Spread in the baking dish.

3. Heat the cream in a small saucepan over medium heat (or in a glass measuring cup in a microwave oven on high) until very hot and steaming. Pour evenly over the vegetables. Cover the dish tightly with aluminum foil and place on a rimmed baking sheet (to catch any cream that might boil over).

4. Bake for 30 minutes. Uncover and bake until the top is golden brown and the vegetables are tender, about 30 minutes longer. Let stand for 5 minutes. Serve hot.

Cranberry Rum-Raisin Sauce

This is another holiday staple that deserves to be served all season long. Cranberries have lots of natural preservatives in them, and this sauce keeps for a few weeks chilled. Make a batch to store in the refrigerator to serve with your turkey, and with pork chops and roasted chicken.

12 ounces cranberries, rinsed and picked over

1 cup packed light brown sugar

1 cup raisins

$\frac{1}{3}$ cup finely chopped crystallized ginger

2 tablespoons balsamic vinegar

$\frac{1}{4}$ cup dark rum

1. Bring the cranberries, brown sugar, raisins, ginger, vinegar, and $\frac{1}{4}$ cup water to a boil in a heavy-bottomed nonreactive medium saucepan over medium-high heat, stirring often to dissolve the sugar. Reduce the heat to medium-low.

2. Simmer uncovered, stirring often, until all the cranberries burst and the juices are syrupy, about 5 minutes. Remove from the heat and stir in the rum. Cool completely. (The sauce can be prepared up to 3 weeks ahead, covered, and refrigerated. Bring to room temperature before serving.)

DESSERTS

Pumpkin Sticky Toffee Pudding

I learned to love sticky pudding during a highly enjoyable trip to Scotland, where almost every menu featured the warm dessert of gooey cake and sauce. It occurred to me that the flavors would take well to an Americanization with pumpkin, and here is the result. It may well be the perfect dessert for an informal autumn gathering, as its beauty lies not in its homey looks, but in its rich flavor.

CAKE

2 cups all-purpose flour

2 teaspoons baking powder

1 teaspoon baking soda

½ teaspoon ground cinnamon

½ teaspoon salt

1 cup (2 sticks) unsalted butter, at room temperature

⅔ cup packed light brown sugar

⅔ cup granulated sugar

4 large eggs, at room temperature

One 15-ounce can solid-pack pumpkin (1¾ cups)

STICKY TOFFEE SAUCE

1 cup packed light brown sugar

8 tablespoons (1 stick) unsalted butter

⅓ cup light corn syrup

1½ cups heavy cream

Sweetened whipped cream, for serving

1. To make the cake, position a rack in the center of the oven and preheat the oven to 350°F. Lightly butter a 13 x 9-inch baking pan.

2. Sift together the flour, baking powder, baking soda, cinnamon, and salt. Beat the butter, brown sugar, and granulated sugar in a large bowl with an electric mixer on high speed until the mixture is light and fluffy, about 3 minutes. One at a time, beat in the eggs. Beat in the pumpkin. If the mixture curdles, do not worry. With the mixer on low speed, beat in the flour mixture in 3 additions, beating until smooth after each addition and scraping down the sides of the bowl as needed. Spread in the baking pan.

3. Bake until a toothpick inserted in the center of the cake comes out clean, 30 to 35 minutes.

4. Meanwhile, make the sticky toffee sauce. Melt the brown sugar, butter, and corn syrup in a heavy-bottomed large saucepan over medium heat, stirring often to help dissolve the sugar. Whisk in the cream and bring to a boil, taking care that the mixture does not boil over. Cook uncovered, whisking often, until the sauce is glossy, smooth, and thick enough to nicely coat a wooden spoon, about 8 minutes. Turn off the burner so the sauce is kept warm by the burner's residual heat.

5. When the cake is done, transfer it to a wire cake rack. Using a meat fork, pierce the cake all over. Pour and spread about 1 cup of the toffee sauce over the cake. Let stand for 10 minutes.

6. Spoon the warm cake into individual bowls, top with more of the warm sauce, and garnish with a dollop of whipped cream. Serve immediately.

Fig Bars

Stuffed with a thick layer of fresh figs and topped with an oat streusel, these scrumptious bars are reminiscent of something you might buy at a top-notch natural food bakery. Wait to make them when figs are abundant and cheap, as you'll need a couple of pounds of the fruit. Nonstick aluminum foil has become one of my favorite new kitchen helpers, as it keeps bar cookies from sticking to the pan and allows the cook to lift out the cooled baked pastry in one piece, then cut it into perfect bars.

FILLING

2¼ pounds ripe dark figs, such as black Mission or Brown Turkey, stems trimmed, fruit coarsely chopped into ¾-inch chunks

¼ cup granulated sugar

Grated zest of ½ lemon

1 tablespoon fresh lemon juice

1 teaspoon cornstarch dissolved in 1 tablespoon cold water

CRUST AND TOPPING

¾ cup packed light brown sugar

6 tablespoons (¾ stick) unsalted butter, plus more for the pan

1 large egg yolk

¾ cup all-purpose flour, plus more for the pan

¾ cup old-fashioned (rolled) oats

¼ teaspoon salt

1. To make the filling, combine the figs, granulated sugar, lemon zest, and lemon juice in a heavy-bottomed medium saucepan. Cover and bring to a simmer over medium heat. Cook, stirring occasionally, until the figs are soft, about 5 minutes. Uncover and cook, stirring often, until the filling is jammy, about 5 minutes more. Stir in the dissolved cornstarch and cook until just thickened, about 30 seconds. Transfer to a bowl and cool completely.

2. Position a rack in the center of the oven and preheat the oven to 350°F. Lightly butter an 8 x 8-inch baking pan. Pleat a 14-inch-long piece of nonstick aluminum foil or parchment paper lengthwise to make an 8-inch-wide strip. Fit into the pan like a sling, pressing the foil into the corners to line the bottom and 2 sides of the pan, and letting the excess hang over the ends to act as handles. Dust the buttered sides of the pan with flour and tap out the excess.

3. To make the crust and topping, beat the brown sugar and butter in a medium bowl with an electric mixer set on high speed until the mixture is light in color, about 1 minute. Beat in the egg yolk. With the mixer on low speed, beat in the flour, oats, and salt to make a soft dough. Set aside 1 cup of the oat mixture for the topping. Press the remaining oat mixture firmly and evenly into the bottom of the foil-lined pan. Spread with the fig filling. Crumble the reserved oat mixture evenly over the fig filling.

4. Bake until the topping is golden brown and the filling is bubbling, about 30 minutes. Transfer to a wire cake rack. Cool completely.

5. Run a knife around the inside of the pan to release the pastry from the sides. Lift up on the foil handles to remove the pastry in one piece from the pan. Cut into 9 bars. (The bars can be stored in an airtight container at room temperature for up to 3 days.)

Figs

Depending on the variety, figs are around throughout the summer. These figs are fine for eating out of hand, but when it comes to cooking with figs, I prefer to wait until the large Brown Turkey figs come into their autumn season. Big and meaty, these figs are less fussy to prepare than the smaller, almost jewel-like black Mission figs or the green Kadotas.

Virtually all of the figs on the market come from California. When I was a kid growing up there, it was a popular backyard crop—in fact, it still is. There always seemed to be more figs than we could eat. I learned early in life that a fig is a somewhat complicated fruit. It can't be casually eaten, like an apple. You have to nibble a ripe fig, as the honeylike juices can dribble faster than you can eat. And beneath its plump skin lie countless tiny seeds that give off a pleasant crunch.

Choose figs that are plump and slightly soft, but not squishy, and they should have an appetizingly sweet aroma. Eating an unripe fig is an exercise in futility. Store them at room temperature for a day or so after purchase, but if they seem to be ripening to the point of spoilage, refrigerate them immediately.

Concord Grape Pie

The earthy flavor of Concord grapes is showcased in this old-fashioned pie. Be forewarned that the grapes must be skinned and strained to make the deep purple filling, but with an extra pair of hands (kids love this chore, especially as the skinned grapes look slightly macabre), it goes very fast. Some recipes make you wonder if the extra effort was worth it. Not this one, which will surely become a new favorite. Serve it with store-bought peanut butter swirl ice cream, and your guests will literally swoon. Mine did.

FILLING

2½ pounds Concord grapes

⅔ cup sugar

¼ cup instant tapioca, ground to a powder in a spice grinder or mini-food processor

2 tablespoons fresh lemon juice

2 tablespoons unsalted butter, thinly sliced

Cream Cheese Pie Dough (page 139)

Ice cream, preferably peanut butter, for serving

1. To make the filling, remove the grapes from the stems; you should have 5 cups. Reserve any extra grapes for another use (like snacking!). Pinch each grape to slip the green flesh out of the purple skin. Reserve the flesh and skins separately. Drain the flesh over a glass bowl, reserving the grape juice.

2. Bring the grape flesh and sugar to a boil in a medium saucepan over medium heat. Cook the grape flesh, stirring often, until it softens, about 5 minutes.

3. Meanwhile, cook the grape juice in the glass bowl in a microwave oven on high, taking care that the bowl is large enough to discourage the juice from boiling over, until the juice is reduced by half, about 5 minutes. (Cooked in a microwave, the juice will reduce without caramelizing. You can also reduce the juice in a saucepan over medium-high heat, but be careful that it doesn't burn. Or skip this step altogether, and add 1/4 cup water or bottled grape juice to the filling.)

4. Pour the grape flesh into a wire sieve over a bowl. Using a rubber spatula, rub the flesh through the sieve, discarding the seeds. Stir in the tapioca, reserved skins, lemon juice, and reduced grape juice. Cool completely. Stir in the butter.

5. Position a rack in the lower third of the oven and preheat the oven to 375°F. Line a rimmed baking sheet with aluminum foil. (This makes for easier cleanup, as the pie is likely to give off juices when it bakes.)

6. On a lightly floured work surface, roll out half of the dough into a 12-inch circle about 1/8 inch thick. Fit into a 9-inch pie pan. Trim the crust flush with the edge of the pan. Spread the filling in the crust. Roll out the remaining dough into a 12-inch circle, and center on top of the filling. Tuck the top crust underneath the bottom crust. Using a fork, press the two crusts together to make a tight seal. Flute the edges of the crusts, if desired. Pierce a center vent and a few slits in the top crust in a decorative pattern with the tip of a small knife.

7. Place the pie on the baking sheet. Bake until the crust is golden brown and the filling can be seen bubbling through the center vent, about 50 minutes. Do not underbake. Transfer to a wire cake rack. Cool completely. Serve at room temperature, with the ice cream.

Concord Grapes

Purple-blue, with a dusty white blush, these big and beautiful grapes are a true American original. They were developed in Concord, Massachusetts, in the mid-1800s to ripen early and avoid the killing frosts. It is a pleasure to picture the botanist Ephraim Wales Bull experimenting with his cuttings surrounded by his literary neighbors Louisa May Alcott, Henry David Thoreau, Nathaniel Hawthorne, and Henry Wadsworth Longfellow.

The flavor of these grapes is most often referred to as foxy (the official scientific name is *Vitus labrusca*, literally "fox grape") or musky, but its richness makes it the perfect grape for jelly. The skins are easy to slip off, but if you are cooking with Concord grapes, the pits are always a bit of a trial to deal with. In spite of the grape's origins in Massachusetts, Washington state now produces the most Concord grapes.

Cream Cheese Pie Dough

Every good baker has his or her favorite piecrust and this one is mine. It bakes up buttery and flaky at the same time, something that isn't easy to accomplish. And it rolls out like the proverbial dream (that is, if you dream about great pie as much as I do). With this dough in your recipe collection, you may find yourself baking pies a lot more often than before.

1 ⅓ cups all-purpose flour

¼ teaspoon salt

10 tablespoons (1 ¼ sticks) unsalted butter, chilled, cut into tablespoons

6 ounces cream cheese (not lowfat), at room temperature, cut into ¾-inch pieces

1. Put the flour and salt in a food processor fitted with the metal chopping blade and pulse to combine them. Add the butter and cream cheese and pulse about 12 times, just until the dough begins to clump together (butter pieces will still be visible). Turn the dough out onto a very lightly floured work surface and gather it together.

2. Divide into 2 disks, and wrap each in plastic wrap. Refrigerate for at least 1 hour or up to 2 days. (If the dough is chilled until it is hard, let it stand at room temperature for about 10 minutes before rolling it out.)

Quince Tarte Tatin

Quince was another harbinger of autumn in California, and my grandmother, like many other cooks, only used to make amber-colored jelly. I learned to turn it into an upside-down tart with a deep rose color. Tarte Tatin is one of the most impressive (and to my mind, one of the easiest, once you get used to flipping the hot tart onto a platter) of all desserts. This isn't very sweet, so feel free to serve ice cream or whipped cream on the side. For the crispest crust, use European-style butter with high butterfat content.

PERFECT BUTTER PASTRY DOUGH

1 cup unbleached all-purpose flour

2 tablespoons sugar

¼ teaspoon salt

8 tablespoons (1 stick) unsalted butter, preferably European style, cut into ½-inch cubes

3 tablespoons ice water, as needed

5 quinces

2 tablespoons fresh lemon juice

4 tablespoons (½ stick) unsalted butter, preferably European style, thinly sliced, divided

¾ cup sugar, divided

1. To make the pastry dough, pulse the flour, sugar, and salt in a food processor fitted with the metal chopping blade to combine. Add the butter and pulse about 8 times until the mixture resembles coarse bread crumbs with some pea-size pieces of butter. Transfer to a bowl. Stir in enough of the ice water to moisten the mixture, just until it begins to clump together (the dough will hold together when pressed between your thumb and forefinger). Gather up into a thick disk and wrap in wax paper. Refrigerate for at least 30 minutes and up to 2 hours.

2. On a lightly floured work surface, roll out the dough into a 12-inch circle about $\frac{1}{8}$ inch thick. Using the skillet lid as a template, cut out a round slightly smaller in circumference than the inside of the skillet. Transfer the dough round to a baking sheet and refrigerate until ready to use.

3. Position a rack in the center of the oven and preheat the oven to 400°F. Have a 9-inch nonstick ovenproof skillet with a domed lid ready.

4. To make the tart, using a vegetable peeler, peel the quinces. Using a paring knife, cut 3 quinces (they are harder than apples, so don't be surprised) lengthwise into quarters, and cut away the hard cores. Cut the remaining 2 quinces lengthwise into eighths, and cut away the hard cores. Transfer to a bowl and toss with the lemon juice.

5. Melt 2 tablespoons of the butter in the skillet over medium heat. Stir in $\frac{1}{3}$ cup plus 1 tablespoon of the sugar. Arrange the quince quarters, curved side down, in a circle in the pan, filling in the empty center with 2 quince quarters. Arrange the quince eighths on top, filling in gaps between the quarters. Sprinkle with the remaining $\frac{1}{3}$ cup plus 1 tablespoon sugar and dot with the remaining 2 tablespoons butter. Cover with the lid. (If your lid doesn't clear the quinces, create a makeshift lid with aluminum foil.) Reduce the heat to medium-low and cook, basting occasionally

with the pan juices (use a bulb baster), until the quinces are just tender when pierced with the tip of a knife, about 12 minutes. Place the pastry round in the skillet, tucking the edges into the skillet.

6. Bake until the pastry is deep golden brown, about 30 minutes. Remove from the oven. Holding the skillet by the handle, give the skillet a gentle shake to be sure that the quinces aren't sticking. Place a flat platter over the skillet. Holding the platter and skillet together, invert them to unmold the tart onto the platter. (Do this quickly and be careful of any hot juices that might escape from the skillet.) Cool for at least 15 minutes. Serve warm or cool to room temperature.

Quinces

In its raw state, quince is not too promising. Looking like a lumpy pear, it is very hard, and wincingly sour and tannic. The only sign of hope is its lovely scent. Cooking quince unlocks its secrets, turning the unwelcoming flesh a rosy pink color with an applelike texture and flavor.

There was always a jar of homemade quince jelly in my grandmother's kitchen cupboard, but I never saw a whole fruit until I became a chef. (I keep a jar in my cupboard, too, not only for toast, but to use as a neutral, sweet-tart, relatively clear glaze for fruit tarts.) Quince is another one of those backyard crops that only recently became commercial.

Buy smooth unblemished quinces that feel heavy for their size, and leave shriveled quinces behind. Fully ripened quince is pale yellow without any tinge of green. If the quince needs ripening, do so at room temperature; you will get a bonus as the fruit gives off a floral aroma during this period. Store the ripe yellow quince in the refrigerator for a week or so. Because quince is so hard, use a large heavy chef's knife to quarter the fruit, then change to a small paring knife to cut out the core with its seeds.

I love cooking with quince, and I often use it in recipes as a substitute for, or in addition to, pears and apples. If you follow my suit, don't forget that the tough quince needs extra time to cook, so give it a head start or cut it into thinner wedges than the other fruits in the recipe.

Carrot-Apple Cupcakes

Cupcakes are back. They are perfect for big parties, as they can be eaten out of hand without utensils or plates and can be easily decorated to suit the occasion. For a Halloween party, color batches of the icing with orange and black food coloring pastes (they give the most intense color), and garnish with colorful candies. For other fall gatherings, leave the icing plain.

CUPCAKES

1 ½ cups all-purpose flour

1 ½ teaspoons baking soda

1 teaspoon ground cinnamon

½ teaspoon freshly grated nutmeg

¼ teaspoon salt

¾ cup granulated sugar

½ cup vegetable oil

¼ cup walnut oil

2 large eggs

2 carrots, peeled and shredded (1 cup)

1 Golden Delicious apple, peeled, cored, and shredded (1 cup)

½ cup dried currants or raisins

½ cup toasted and coarsely chopped walnuts

ICING

4 ounces (half of an 8-ounce package) cream cheese, at room temperature

1 ½ cups confectioners' sugar, sifted

1 teaspoon fresh lemon juice

1. Position an oven rack in the center of the oven and preheat the oven to 350°F. Line the cups of a 12-cup muffin pan with paper cupcake liners.

2. To make the cupcakes, sift together the flour, baking soda, cinnamon, nutmeg, and salt. Mix the granulated sugar, vegetable and walnut oils, and eggs with an electric mixer on high speed until the mixture is a shade paler, about 1 minute. Stir in the flour mixture, then the carrots and apples. Fold in the currants and walnuts. Using an ice cream scoop, divide the batter evenly among the muffin cups.

3. Bake until a toothpick inserted in the centers of the cupcakes comes out clean, about 20 minutes. Let the cupcakes stand in the muffin pan for 5 minutes, then transfer to a wire rack to cool completely.

4. To make the icing, place the cheese in a medium bowl. Using an electric mixer on low speed, gradually beat in the confectioners' sugar, working it into the cheese until the icing is smooth. Beat in the lemon juice.

5. Spread the icing over the tops of the cupcakes. Serve at room temperature.

Meyer Lemon–Pistachio Bars

If I were forced to make a choice of my favorite cookie, lemon bars would make the very short list. When Meyer lemons showed up unexpectedly at the produce market, I immediately ran home and created this irresistible variation to showcase the perfumelike aroma and gentle tang of the lemons. A pistachio crust adds even more elegance.

PISTACHIO CRUST

¾ cup all-purpose flour

½ cup shelled pistachios

¼ cup confectioners' sugar

⅛ teaspoon salt

7 tablespoons (¾ stick plus 1 tablespoon) unsalted butter, at room temperature

¼ teaspoon pistachio or almond extract (see Note)

MEYER LEMON FILLING

1 cup granulated sugar

3 large eggs

Grated zest of 2 lemons, preferably Meyer lemons

⅓ cup fresh lemon juice, preferably from Meyer lemons

¾ teaspoon baking powder

¼ teaspoon salt

1. Position a rack in the center of the oven and preheat the oven to 350°F. Lightly butter an 8 x 8-inch baking pan. Pleat a 14-inch-long piece of nonstick aluminum foil or parchment paper lengthwise to make an 8-inch-wide strip. Fit into a pan like a sling,

pressing the foil into the corners to line the bottom and 2 sides of the pan, letting the excess hang over the ends to act as handles. Dust the buttered sides of the pan with flour and tap out the excess.

2. To make the crust, process the flour, pistachios, confectioners' sugar, and salt in a food processor fitted with the metal chopping blade until the pistachios are very finely ground, about 30 seconds. Add the butter and pistachio extract and pulse until the mixture begins to clump together. Transfer to the pan. Press the pistachio dough firmly and evenly into the bottom of the pan. Bake until the crust is set and lightly browned around the edges, 12 to 15 minutes.

3. To make the filling, whisk together the sugar, eggs, lemon zest and juice, baking powder, and salt until well blended. Pour into the crust and bake until the filling is set and golden brown, 20 to 25 minutes. Transfer to a wire cake rack and cool completely.

4. Run a sharp knife around the inside of the pan to release the pastry. Pull up on the foil handles to remove the pasty in one piece. Sift confectioners' sugar over the top. Cut into 9 bars and serve. (The bars can be made up to 2 days ahead, covered, and refrigerated.)

Note

Pistachio extract can be purchased at specialty food stores with a large selection of cooking flavor extracts, or online at www.jacksonvillemercantile.com, www.saffron.com, and www.silvercloudestates.com.

Meyer Lemons

After I moved to New York in my twenties, I had to get used to buying lemons. In California, I always had a friend or relative who was trying to unload another bumper crop from their tree. But, invariably, the lemons were of the tart, thick-skinned Eureka lemon variety. They were classically puckery, and many a young entrepreneur in my neighborhood sold pitchers of lemonade made from the family tree.

In the last few years, another lemon has appeared, threatening the supremacy of the Eureka. This is the perfumed, thin-skinned, neon-yellow Meyer lemon, a cross between a traditional lemon and a tangerine. Introduced to the United States from China in 1908, they never were a huge crop, but they had their fans. Then it was discovered that the trees carried a destructive citrus virus, and in order to preserve the other millions of trees so valuable to California's economy, all Meyers in the United States were destroyed. It wasn't until 1975 that a disease-resistant tree was released to nurseries, and this tree returned to backyards in California, Florida, and Texas. When chefs started cooking with the slightly less acidic Meyer lemons, its popularity was virtually guaranteed.

For many years, the only way I could cook with Meyer lemons was during fall trips home. Now, commercial crops are being grown, and I can buy Meyers at the natural-foods supermarket five minutes from my house in New Jersey. Old-guard Californian cooks (i.e., my parents and their gardener friends) still love their Eurekas, and they complain that Meyers aren't tart enough. I say there's room for both.

Pumpkin Hazelnut Bars

When you're asked to bring dessert to an autumn potluck, these pumpkin pie squares should be on your short list of possible recipes. Baking and transporting a few pumpkin pies is no small feat, but this big pan of bars with a crisp hazelnut crust and creamy-spicy filling is a snap. If you wish, top each square with a rosette of whipped cream and a sprinkle of minced crystallized ginger.

HAZELNUT CRUST

1 cup all-purpose flour

½ cup toasted and coarsely chopped hazelnuts (see Note)

¼ teaspoon salt

8 tablespoons (1 stick) unsalted butter, at room temperature

½ cup packed light brown sugar

FILLING

One 15-ounce can solid-pack pumpkin

¾ cup packed light brown sugar

2 large eggs

1 teaspoon ground cinnamon

½ teaspoon salt

½ teaspoon ground ginger

¼ teaspoon ground cloves

1 ½ cups heavy cream

1. Position a rack in the lower third of the oven and preheat the oven to 350°F. Lightly butter a 13 x 9-inch baking pan. Pleat a 22-inch-long piece of nonstick aluminum foil or parchment paper lengthwise to make a 9-inch-wide strip. Fit into the pan like a sling,

pressing the foil into the corners to line the bottom and 2 sides of the pan, and letting the excess hang over the ends to act as handles. Dust the buttered sides of the pan with flour and tap out the excess.

2. To make the crust, combine the flour, hazelnuts, and salt in a food processor fitted with the metal chopping blade. Process until the nuts are ground into a powder, about 20 seconds.

3. Beat the butter and brown sugar in a medium bowl with an electric mixer set on high speed until the mixture is pale, about 1 minute. With the mixer on low speed, mix in the flour mixture to make a soft dough. Press the dough firmly and evenly into the bottom of the foil-lined pan. Bake the dough until it looks set and is beginning to brown around the edges, about 15 minutes.

4. To make the filling, whisk together the pumpkin, brown sugar, eggs, cinnamon, salt ginger, and cloves in a medium bowl to dissolve the sugar. Gradually whisk in the cream.

5. Remove the crust from the oven and pour in the filling. Return to the oven. Bake until the filling is set in the center when the pan is gently shaken, about 35 minutes. Transfer to a wire cake rack and cool completely.

6. Run a knife around the inside of the pan to release the pastry. Lift up on the foil handles to remove the pastry in one piece from the pan. Cut into 24 bars. (The bars can be covered and refrigerated for up to 3 days.) Serve chilled or at room temperature.

Note

To toast and peel hazelnuts, spread the hazelnuts on a rimmed baking sheet. Bake in a preheated 350°F oven, stirring occasionally, until the hazelnuts' skins are cracked, 12 to 15 minutes. Transfer to a kitchen towel and let stand for a few minutes. Wrap the nuts in the towel and use the towel as an aide to rub off the skins. Do not worry about removing every bit of skin. Cool completely.

Apple Kuchen

My dear friend Elizabeth Kilbert has been making this deep-dish apple kuchen for years. You may find yourself preferring it to apple pie. It keeps for a few days, even unrefrigerated, and you will find that it is not only a wonderful dessert after dinner but also a terrific breakfast. A silicone rolling pin will help when rolling out the sugary dough. Don't fret if the dough cracks; just piece it back together, as this is supposed to be a rustic dish.

DOUGH

8 tablespoons (1 stick) unsalted butter, at room temperature

½ cup vegetable shortening

1 cup sugar

1 large egg plus 1 large egg yolk

1 teaspoon vanilla extract

1 teaspoon salt

3½ cups all-purpose flour

6 Golden Delicious apples, peeled, cored, and thinly sliced

½ cup sugar

2 tablespoons fresh lemon juice

2 teaspoons cinnamon

1 large egg yolk

1 tablespoon whole milk

1. To make the dough, mix the butter, shortening, and sugar in a medium bowl with an electric mixer on high speed until the mixture is light in color and texture, about 3 minutes. Reduce the mixer speed to low and beat in the egg and yolk, vanilla, and salt. Gradually mix in the flour to make a soft dough. Gather up the dough and divide into two portions, one about twice as big as the other. Shape each dough portion into a thick rectangle and wrap in plastic wrap. Refrigerate until chilled, at least 2 hours and up to 4 hours. (The dough is easiest to work with when it is chilled, but not rock hard.)

2. Position a rack in the center of the oven and preheat the oven to 350°F. Using unsalted butter, lightly butter a 13 x 9-inch baking dish.

3. Mix the apples, sugar, lemon juice, and cinnamon in a medium bowl. On a lightly floured work surface, roll out the larger portion of dough into a rectangle about 17 x 13 inches. Starting at a short end, roll up the dough onto the rolling pin, and unroll the dough over the baking dish. Fit the dough into the dish. Pour in and spread out the apples. Roll out the smaller portion of dough into a 13 x 9-inch rectangle and fit over the apples. Pinch the edges of the dough together. Cut a few slits in the top crust. Mix together the egg yolk and milk in a small bowl, and brush some of the mixture over the top crust.

4. Place the dish on a rimmed baking sheet. Bake until the kuchen is golden brown, about 1¼ hours. Transfer the dish to a wire cake rack and cool completely.

Apples

Of all of autumn's bounty, apples are probably the fruit most closely identified with the season. In the Western Hemisphere, they are in season from the last days of summer all the way through the early weeks of winter—and then, thanks to cold storage, they are available long after that. Apples can be grown in cool regions because the trees don't blossom until late spring, and loss from frost is diminished. So, it's no wonder that autumn cooking is filled with apples.

The old adage "as American as apple pie" is not entirely true, as the apple tree originated in Asia Minor (now eastern Turkey) and apple pie was a staple in England before the recipe traveled here with the Pilgrims. With more than 100 apple varieties grown commercially in the United States, one of the most common cooking questions is "Which apples are best for apple pie?"

An apple's main flavor characteristics are sweet or tart. When it comes to texture, most cooks believe that an apple that holds its shape after cooking is preferable to one that turns mushy. After baking countless apple pies, for the most reliable results I recommend Golden Delicious apples, with their honeyed sweetness and firm texture. When I make my deep-dish Apple Kuchen (page 153), I never stray from this variety. Don't discredit Golden Delicious apples just because they are ubiquitous; my farmers' market has a local crop that

is great. I am not a fan of Granny Smith apples, for while they may have a tart edge that works well in pie, they become gray when cooked. Apples that turn soft during baking, such as McIntosh or Red Delicious, should also be avoided. Although you will find plenty of cooks who think that the best apple pie is one that is made from a mixture of apple varieties—mixing sugary and sour, firm and soft—such a conglomeration is difficult to sweeten and spice confidently.

But the best way to find the perfect apple for your pie (or for eating, or for cooking alongside a pork roast, for that matter) is to ask the producers at your farmers' market or farm stand. They may have a treasure that you are unfamiliar with, just waiting to be tucked between crusts to make a wonderful pie.

Pear-Cranberry Crisp

Makes 6 to 8 servings

Spooning up a heaping portion of warm fruit crisp is an autumn ritual right up there with carving the Halloween jack-o'-lantern. This crisp matches tart cranberries with sweet pears. Be sure to buy a juicy pear variety such as Anjou or Bartlett instead of the drier Bosc. And be patient with the baking, as it takes time for the thick layer of oat topping to truly become crisp.

One 12-ounce bag fresh cranberries, rinsed and picked over

1½ cups packed light brown sugar, divided

4 ripe pears, peeled, cored, and cut into 1-inch chunks

¼ cup all-purpose flour

2 tablespoons fresh lemon juice

1 teaspoon pumpkin pie spice, or ½ teaspoon each ground ginger and ground cinnamon

2 tablespoons unsalted butter, cut into small cubes

TOPPING

1 cup old-fashioned (rolled) oats

¾ cup packed light brown sugar

½ cup all-purpose flour

¼ teaspoon salt

8 tablespoons (1 stick) unsalted butter, cut up, at room temperature

Vanilla ice cream, for serving

1. Position a rack in the center of the oven and preheat the oven to 375°F. Lightly butter an 11 ½ x 8-inch baking dish.

Desserts

157

2. Combine the cranberries and 1 cup of the brown sugar in a medium saucepan. Bring to a simmer over medium heat, stirring often to dissolve the sugar. Cook until the cranberries burst, about 5 minutes. Pour into the prepared dish. Let stand to cool until tepid, about 15 minutes.

3. Mix together the pears, the remaining ½ cup of brown sugar, the flour, lemon juice, and pumpkin pie spice. Pour over the cranberries and dot with the butter.

4. To make the topping, mix together the oats, brown sugar, flour, and salt in a bowl. Add the butter and rub everything together with your fingers until combined. Press the mixture together into a cohesive mass. Crumble in a relatively even layer over the pears. Place on a rimmed baking sheet (to catch any bubbling juices).

5. Bake until the juices are bubbling and the topping is crisp, 50 to 60 minutes. Cool until warm, and serve with the ice cream.

Grandma Edith's Persimmon Cookies

Makes about 2 ½ dozen

You may have heard it from friends: "I wish that I had asked Grandma for her recipe!" Happily, I have no such remorse, and I asked both of my grandmothers (and great-aunts, too) for their best recipes. Growing up in California, we had many neighbors with big persimmon trees, and there was no shortage of recipes that used the gorgeous fruit. To this day, I can't wait until persimmons hit the market in October so I can make a batch of these soft, spicy cookies.

2 very soft, ripe Hachiya persimmons

2 cups all-purpose flour

1 teaspoon baking soda

½ teaspoon ground cinnamon

½ teaspoon freshly grated nutmeg

½ teaspoon ground cloves

¼ teaspoon salt

8 tablespoons (1 stick) unsalted butter, at room temperature

1 cup sugar

1 large egg, at room temperature

1 cup coarsely chopped walnuts

1. Position racks in the top third and center of the oven and preheat the oven to 350°F. Lightly butter 2 baking sheets, or line them with silicone baking mats or parchment paper.

2. Coarsely chop the fruit, discarding the calyxes and any seeds. Puree the persimmons in a food processor fitted with the metal blade or in a blender. You should have 1 cup.

3. Sift together the flour, baking soda, cinnamon, nutmeg, cloves, and salt. Using an electric mixer set at high speed, cream the butter and sugar, scraping down the sides of the bowl as needed, until the mixture is light and fluffy, about 3 minutes. Beat in the egg. With the mixer on low speed, beat in the persimmon puree, then the flour mixture. Stir in the nuts.

4. Using 1 tablespoon for each cookie, drop the dough, 2 inches apart, on the baking sheets. Bake, switching the positions of the sheets from front to back and from top to bottom halfway through baking, until the edges of the cookies are lightly browned, about 15 minutes. Transfer to wire cake racks and cool completely.

Index